RICHARD MONTGOMERY

Rebel of 1775

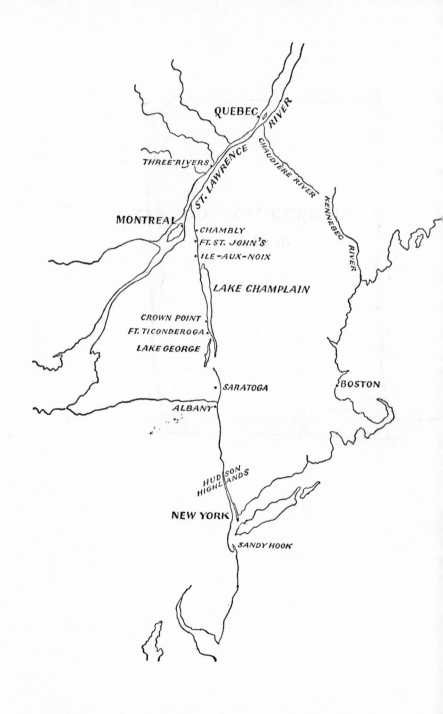

RICHARD MONTGOMERY

Rebel of 1775

by A. L. TODD

Maps and decoration by Leonard Vosburgh

DAVID McKAY COMPANY, Inc.   NEW YORK

RICHARD MONTGOMERY—REBEL OF 1775

COPYRIGHT © 1966 BY A. L. TODD

LIBRARY OF CONGRESS CATALOG CARD NUMBER: 67-17532

MANUFACTURED IN THE UNITED STATES OF AMERICA

VAN REES PRESS • NEW YORK

Typography by Charles M. Todd

PREFACE

THE EVENTS in these pages are matters of historical record. In a few places I have concluded what must have happened in logical sequence between known facts supported by documents. A number of melodramatic touches that have been used to color various accounts of General Richard Montgomery's life are omitted from this book, either because they have been proved wrong, or because they rest on sources so doubtful that an honest account should not credit them as true. Nothing has been fictionalized; this story is not dressed in the cloak of invention to add luster to the facts. I believe that the factual account of America's first national war hero of high rank to die in her struggle for freedom can stand on its own.

—A. L. Todd
New York City, 1966

Contents

Contents

1

New York—A City Divided

IN THE third week of May in 1775, as Richard Mont-gomery rode down the Hudson River Valley to attend the Provincial Congress, New York was a city, and a province, passionately divided against itself.

The people of New York had not waited that year for the bright sunshine of May, following the chill winds and rain of early spring, to lure them out of doors. For the spring of 1775 was like no other that any man could remember. It was a time of suspense and tension, of strained tempers and angry words, of rumors flying with express speed, of both good news and bad, of fist-shaking argument and boisterous shouting as tankards clanged on tavern tables.

The freeborn English colonists of New York could stand no more bad government from London. They were in no way opposed to King George III, nor to the idea of British government, for they were loyal subjects of the British crown. Rather, their anger was directed against the clique of politicians who had taken hold of the British Parliament and voted themselves into power as the king's ministers.

One oppressive ministry had succeeded another in the last decade. Among the ministers a few faces would change from year to year, but their anti-colonial policies remained the same, or got worse.

It was twelve years now since the end of the war against the French in 1763. In that struggle the men of the American colonies had fought bravely and well at the side of the regular troops from the mother country. Many of them had fallen in the war that had cleared the soldiers of the king of France from their base to the north, in Canada. Since that victory all of North America had been safe for the colonists of Great Britain.

But instead of being treated like good and loyal subjects of His Majesty King George, with rights equal to those of men living in England, the American colonists were being saddled with oppressive restrictions on their commerce as if they were a conquered people. In recent years the ministry had imposed ever larger bodies of troops on New York and the other colonies along the Atlantic coast to enforce the collection of taxes. The charges of maintaining the troops were also put on the shoulders of the American provinces. The burden was becoming heavier, yet the tax money extracted from the colonists was not being used for their welfare or protection. It was being taken overseas to pay for the follies and errors of corrupt politicians of the Tory faction who infested the Parliament and who had taken control of the government. Furthermore, it was a Parliament in which American colonists had no representatives, and therefore no voice.

By the spring of 1775, there was a spirit of defiance hovering thick in the air. In New York the traditional Englishman's respect for the officers and agents of the crown had disappeared. In its place had grown a deep, resentful hostility, that was now shouted brazenly in street, shop and tavern. It came to the lips of merchant and artisan and farmer, as he assailed the tax collector with a stream of abuse, punctuated with such words as "outrage," "tyranny" and "iniquity." Red-coated soldiers in the streets felt its sting, as ragamuffin boys darted out from alleyways to pelt them with snowballs or pebbles, according to the season, then disappeared as fast as their legs could carry them. British army officers experienced it as the doors of some of the leading houses, once graciously opened to their visits, now remained coldly closed when they called.

Nor was rebellion festering in New York alone. A like stirring of emotions was felt in every city in the colonies, from Portland and Portsmouth down the coast to Charleston and Savannah. British government officials and their immediate followers were forced to draw apart from their neighbors. Those few who held offices of profit under the crown, or who through some perverse notion of blind loyalty to the British government did not see any cause to protest, were scornfully labeled Tories by the other colonists—after the Tory party that controlled Parliament in the mother country. They were the ones who had a stake in continuing things as they were, or who believed that resistance to the ministerial troops would lead a troublemaker directly to prison, or to the gallows. But the Tories were the few.

The dominant mood of the people of New York was one of defiance. In every quarter of town, men were talking openly of "resisting" the troops and "fighting for liberty." Such talk came from men who were the backbone of the city and the province of New York. Among them were the most prosperous merchants, the lawyers, the skilled artisans and tradesmen whose workshops had made the city a bustling, prosperous center of commerce. Elsewhere in the colony it was much the same. In the minds of the people in the towns and villages of the vast hinterland of the province stretching up the Hudson River Valley, New York City had supplanted England as the center of trade and civilization. New York was their London, the one big town they visited in their life span.

Among the most defiant were the farmers, tens upon tens of thousands of them, who had spread out in the American provinces over a territory many times the size of Britain. These were men who rejoiced in the freedom to till their own soil, or who hoped soon to buy their own land when their period of indenture would be over. They had won this land with ax and musket and plow, and detested every sign of the landlord system of the Old World. Such men did not easily part with one shilling they had earned from their own hard labor, if they thought it was being unjustly taken.

It was the third week in April that year when news from Massachusetts aroused New York to a fighting mood. Express riders carried dispatches from the sister colony telling of the outbreak of musket-fire between a detachment of British regulars and the townsmen and farmers a few miles west of Boston. The Americans had tried to prevent the British soldiery from seizing a large store of gunpowder that the colonists had placed at Concord. The colonials had actually taken up arms and had fired on the soldiers over a period of many hours, killing a number of them. And although the regulars had the better of the fight by the time they had returned to the city with most of the powder, they had suffered severe losses.

Snowballs and insults on an individual basis had been

one thing; but a clash involving hundreds of armed men was quite another. The fights at Concord and Lexington were clear acts of armed rebellion, and most people in and around Boston applauded the insurrectionists and supported them. New Yorkers learned that the British commander, General Thomas Gage, was now virtually a prisoner in Boston. He was penned with his troops in the narrow peninsula on which the old North End of Boston was clustered, because the nearby countryside was no longer safe territory for him or his men.

To the people of New York, the parallel between their town and Boston was obvious. Like Boston, New York was built on a point that jutted out into a natural harbor protected from the ocean waves, where ships of commerce and of war by the dozens could safely cast anchor close to shore. New York, like Boston, had grown into an important city as the province inland from the port expanded in population. Now it was the focal point of a large colony, the gateway for men and merchandise arriving in America from the British homeland, and for exports. It had grown into a center of genteel social life and of politics. In the past few years, as nearly as the tax officers could reckon, the town of New York with its 22,000 inhabitants had passed both Boston and Philadelphia in population and had become the largest city in British America.

Originally a Dutch town called New Amsterdam in the early sixteen hundreds, New York had been taken by a British naval force in 1664 during the war between Britain and the Netherlands. In the century that had passed since New Amsterdam became New York, the town had become thoroughly English. Indeed, the signs of its Dutch origin were now observed mainly in the design of the oldest houses, in place names like the Harlem River to the east of York Island, and in family names such as Schuyler, Van Rensselaer and Roosevelt. The dominant church was the Anglican, or Church of England. The newspapers were modeled on those printed in England, the people bought and sold merchandise by the British system of pounds, shillings and pence.

Most important, the people of New York, like their fellow Americans in Boston, Philadelphia, Baltimore and elsewhere, looked upon themselves as Englishmen, who were living on the American continent. England's king was their king, their suits were tried in the king's courts, the laws of Britain were their laws. Furthermore, their literature, customs and manners, their heroes and ideals were the same as those of the British Isles.

It was the very fact that they were Englishmen that caused the American colonists to resent the unfair treatment being dealt them by a ministry which they had no voice in choosing. It was as though they had been cheated of almost all the precious liberties that Englishmen had won in the course of the long struggle against the tyranny of the Stuart kings in the previous century. Merchants and manufacturers in the mother country could trade freely among each other, and the British navy enforced their right to carry on commerce overseas. The American colonists, on the other hand, were bound by restrictions against trading directly with one another. They were commanded to trade only as the mother country directed—and for the profit of the mother country, not their own or that of their neighbors in America. Moreover, British military power was employed to enforce the restrictions.

Englishmen living in London, Newcastle, Bristol and

Plymouth had representatives in Parliament, who could at least reach the ear of the king's ministers. New Yorkers and Bostonians, however, had no representatives in Parliament or at court. The royal governor of the province of New York was appointed from London. He was placed there to impose the ministry's will on the people of New York, using force where necessary. If he grew rich from the office, as appointed governors generally did, he was resented all the more. The governor and his troops personified government by oppression, not by consent, for the benefit of corrupt politicians far away.

The city of New York lay on the southern tip of a long, thin island which the Dutch had termed Manhattan, after its Indian name. The English sometimes called it Manhattan, but more often referred to it as York Island. Extending about fourteen miles northward from the city, its surface dotted with sharp outcroppings of granite, abrupt hills, rolling meadowland, woodland and swamp, York Island was separated from the mainland at its upper end by a narrow, swift-running creek that reversed course with the tides. Along the west shore of the island, stretching northward as far as one could see, lay the mighty North River, also known after its discoverer as Hudson's River. This inviting waterway was navigable to ocean-going schooners for one hundred and fifty miles upstream. It was the fact of such an inland waterway connecting with the large, well-protected harbor that made this a natural place for the growth of a port city.

The town itself covered an area roughly triangular in shape, measuring nearly a mile and a half on each side. It came to a focus at the southern tip of the island where Fort George, its solid stonework walls bristling with cannon, stood like a sentinel looking down the harbor. Two sides of the triangle led northeast and northwest from Fort George like a wide letter V, along the shores of the Hudson and the East rivers. Quays and docks marked the waterfront of both rivers almost as far as streets and houses had been built. Near the docks the masts and spars of ships in berth or riding at anchor mingled in thick profusion, like the tangled branches of a wood in winter after the wind has stripped them bare of leaves.

Upward on York Island between the angle formed by the two waterfront sides of the town, New York since its Dutch settlement days had been steadily extending into the meadows and woods, as its population grew and people required room for homes and shops. Wall Street, so named after the protective wooden wall that had once marked the northern boundary of the old Dutch town, now cut across the middle of the city. New streets were being opened and stone pavements laid as the town expanded. A stagecoach had operated between Boston and New York since 1772, its terminus being Fowler's Tavern at Fresh Water, a pond lying on the northern outskirts of town. The route to the country inland led north along Broad Way, curving right into Bowery Lane, and then turning slightly to the left at the edge of the city. Here it became the Post Road to Albany and Boston. Winding through farms and woodland for about ten miles, the Post Road skirted low-lying marshes and the steepest of York Island's hills, crossed a number of creeks, then led steadily upward as it approached the rocky meadows on the upper end of the island.

At the top of a long grade, about ten miles from town, a traveler from New York would find it convenient to stop at the Blue Bell, a small, hospitable tavern where he could drink and dine while the horses were being watered and rested. From the summit of a hill behind the Blue Bell, about two hundred yards across a slanting meadow to the northwest, one could obtain a magnificent view of the surrounding countryside. This vantage point was the highest spot on Manhattan Island. From it one could look directly west to the craggy cliffs on the far shore of Hudson's River. Washing the base of these sheer palisades of rock, the majestic Hudson led like a broad highway southward down to New York harbor and to the sea, and in the other direction into the heart of the North American continent.

Only with a very sharp eye on a clear day could one make out the highest spires of New York beyond the rolling hills that lay between the viewer and the town. But in the foreground one could discern any number of farmhouses, with fields, hedges and orchards, some of them clustered in hamlets such as Harlem and Bloomingdale, that dated back to the days of the settlers from the Netherlands. To the north from this hilltop one could view the mainland of the province. It was reached by way of King's Bridge, which crossed the narrow Harlem Kill some two miles above the Blue Bell. Here at King's Bridge the road divided. Travelers for the Hudson Valley towns would bear to the left and north, whereas those bound for Connecticut and Boston took the Post Road eastward to the right.

Everywhere hereabouts the land was good, and those who lived on it had prospered. Fields, meadows and orchards yielded fine harvests, game abounded in the meadowland and forest, and rivers and bays ran heavy with fish. New York Province was in every way a country of plenty for those who would work to cultivate its natural bounty.

The fact that New York was rich and growing only added

to the anger of the colonists against the outrages imposed on them by the king's ministers. In 1765 the government had tried to raise revenue from the colonies by a stamp tax, requiring that every legal and commercial paper bear a stamp, which those doing any kind of business would be required to buy. The stamp tax had enraged virtually the entire population of New York and other centers of commerce, to the point where delegates from nine British colonies had assembled in New York to protest against it. In New York City the stamps had been kept in Fort George under armed guard and were never even put in circulation, for fear of their being destroyed by outraged citizens. The ministry, sensing the mood of the colonies, hastily repealed the stamp tax within a year.

From that point on, there were frequent clashes between agents of the crown and citizens of New York. A committee of the most active men formed an association called the Sons of Liberty, whose members erected a "Liberty Pole" near Fort George as a symbol of their determination to resist tyranny. The British military, seeing the liberty pole as a sign of defiance of their authority, cut it down, as they did several more poles that the New Yorkers raised to replace those destroyed by the troops. At length a violent dispute between the soldiery and a group of angry New Yorkers broke out on Golden Hill, a slanting street near the East River docks, and led to the troops using their bayonets to drive away the crowd. Meanwhile, similar acts of defiance and physical clashes had taken place in Boston, where a cargo of British-owned tea was dumped into the harbor, and where in 1770 troops on Boston Common fired into a hostile crowd, killing five men.

It was therefore against a background of years of in-

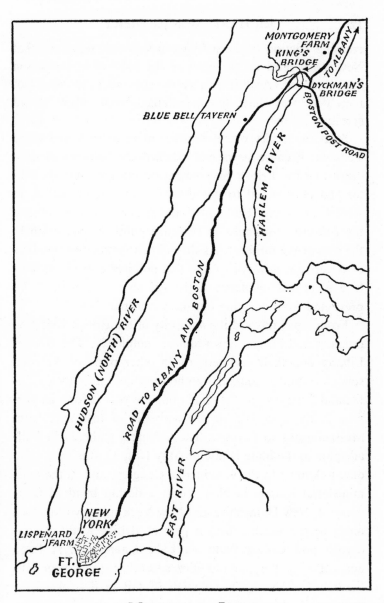

MANHATTAN ISLAND

creasing friction between king's troops and populace that New York received the news of the fighting at Lexington and Concord. And it was easily seen that this was not merely a local clash, but a sustained battle. More would certainly follow.

Such outbreaks would become more serious and more frequent, because news had reached the colonies in mid-April that the British government during the previous winter had determined to put down all show of rebellion in America by force. Undaunted, the leaders of protest among the colonists continued to organize political opposition to the acts of the ministry. As they did so, increasing numbers of Americans now recognized that political opposition must lead to armed resistance if the British troops were to be prevented from carrying out the government's will.

From April onward the authority of the British civil government had broken down almost completely. The Sons of Liberty and their counterparts in other parts of America sought common counsel by choosing delegates to a Continental Congress, as they had done the year before, its purpose being to coordinate the activities of resistance from Massachusetts to Georgia. The Congress gathered in Philadelphia at the State House on May 10th. On the very same day, unknown to the Continental Congress and to the anti-ministerial leaders in New York, a daring band of Connecticut, New Hampshire and New York men two hundred miles to the north seized a pair of British forts—Ticonderoga and Crown Point on Lake Champlain. A large amount of artillery, ammunition and other stores came into the hands of the armed colonials by this bold stroke. In a measure it redressed the balance lost in the skirmishing around Concord three weeks before. Now the colonists had the means with which to fight in earnest.

In early May, word was dispatched to all parts of New York that delegates to a Provincial Assembly, or Congress, should be chosen by election, to meet in New York City on Monday, May 22nd. The royal governor of the province, William Tryon, had been absent in England for most of the previous year. His deputy governor, Cadwallader Colden, had completely lost any control over events in city and province. The handful of regular troops were kept close to their quarters in Fort George. Governor Tryon's official council enjoyed almost no respect in the colony, except from the handful of Tories who continued to profess their loyalty to the government.

The Provincial Assembly, although an unofficial body, already was assuming a shadowy kind of dual authority to that of the colonial government. It was conceived as a parliament for the majority of New Yorkers, and would derive its power from the fact that it would reflect the will of determined people who were in physical control of the streets and the countryside. It was not intended as a government. Yet it would be the only body that could speak for the people of New York, since the authority once wielded by ministry, governor and soldiery had diminished practically to nothing.

It was toward a city thus divided between bold rebel and hesitant Tory, between the fading authority of British government and the rising influence of the Continental Congress, that Richard Montgomery made his way, just after the middle of May in 1775. As he crossed King's Bridge to York Island, and later as he looked out over the land stretched before him from the height by the Blue Bell tavern,

Montgomery must have already been thinking ahead to a plan under which New York should be prepared to fight for this vital ground.

Montgomery had been a soldier most of his adult life. He was newly settled in America, but this part of the country he knew of old. His service during the late war against the French as an officer in the British army, and particularly his experiences along this strategic highway comprising the Hudson River, Lake George and Lake Champlain, which led directly into the Province of Quebec, prepared him to look on this as more than a travel route. It was a potential battleground of major importance. For should armed hostilities between the British troops and the colonists become general, this line of the Hudson and the lakes must be defended. If the British were to take possession of it, and hold it in sufficient strength, they could then control all the northern colonies from New York to Quebec.

There was another, more personal, reason for holding the Hudson, beyond the purely strategic plans fomulating in Montgomery's mind. His own home and land lay close to the Hudson River in Dutchess County, seventy miles above New York City. He had a wife and many friends dear to him in the towns and estates nearby. A number of gentlemen had already spoken to Montgomery of his duty to act as a leader, since he had acquired more military experience at age thirty-six than almost any other man in the province. There was no colonial army yet in being. Nor was there, as of this day, a general war. But it appeared inevitable that there would be war, and that he would be summoned.

Fate, it seemed, was reaching out for Richard Montgomery, with the melancholy command that he take up the sword against his former comrades-in-arms.

❧ 2 ❧

Mr. Montgomery of Dutchess County

M ONDAY, May 22nd, was the day appointed for the opening of the New York Provincial Congress. The scheduled place was the Exchange, a large commercial building at the foot of Broad Street next to the docks on the East River, within a hundred yards of the south harbor battery flanking Fort George. The Exchange had been established more than a century before as a meeting place for ships' masters and the merchants of the city. Here, since 1670, the men who did the business of the port bought, sold and bargained for cargoes. Within its walls they exchanged the gold and silver monies of Spain, France, Holland, England and other lands beyond the seas.

When the appointed day came, only a few of the deputies chosen by the outlying counties had reached the city, so the first meeting was postponed for a day, until May 23d. When the New York Provincial Congress was called to order, sixty-three men were present of more than eighty whose election in the ten counties of the province had been certified. Twenty of them represented New York City itself.

During the first two days of meetings the total was increased by the arrival of more deputies, wearied by long, hard riding from distant parts of the colony.

The New York Congress had no time to lose. Fighting had begun and decisions must be made. As the deputies listened to the first urgent piece of business read out for their consideration, these substantial British colonial gentlemen must have sensed that they were coming close to actual warfare with the mother country. It was clear from the start that this assembly was not to be a mere debating society. Rather, it was a council for action. When Richard Montgomery reached the hall for the May 24th session, he learned that the New York Congress had already decided to accept a grave responsibility assigned to it by the Continental Congress, then meeting in Philadelphia.

One week earlier, the Continental Congress had been startled to learn of the seizure of the two British strongpoints, Crown Point and Fort Ticonderoga, which lay on the west shore of Lake Champlain near its southern end. Though unexpected, the news was warmly welcome to many of the patriots. Without delay, the delegates in Philadelphia had decided that the cannon and military stores that had fallen into the hands of the irregular Continental forces by this bold coup in the north must be safeguarded from seizure by the regular British troops. The redcoats already had too much power in the colonies.

The two Champlain forts had been captured by a mixed lot of men from Connecticut, New Hampshire and New York. Most of them were rough woodsmen and farmers loosely formed into a regional militia. They called themselves the Green Mountain Boys, and had chosen as their captain a daring, flamboyant fellow named Ethan Allen.

Also present as a secondary leader at the attack was a widely traveled, fast-talking Connecticut man, a dealer in horses, cloth and medicines named Benedict Arnold. The great advantage of the raiders had been the complete surprise with which they had rushed upon Fort Ticonderoga in the early morning, when the garrison was unaware that any armed men were within miles of the place. And Crown Point, just ten miles away, had been manned by not much more than a sergeant's guard. Indeed, taking the two points had been little more than a glorified prank carried out by grown men with muskets.

But the matter of securing the military stores they had seized was a serious business, which the Continental Congress urged the New York body to undertake without losing a day. None of the New York leaders had known of the plans for the Arnold-Allen raid until after it had taken place. Yet since both forts lay within New York Province, the New York Congress would have to furnish the men to remove the stores and to garrison both strongpoints. This was so for two reasons. First, most of the irregular groups of men under arms in the New England colonies were now being drawn toward Boston, where volunteers with muskets were urgently needed. Second, New York had the transportation route along which the heavy load of cannon, shot and powder could be moved to a position of relative safety from the British.

Manpower, wagons and boats and the money to secure them quickly were all required. The task involved moving the stores across a short neck of land that separated Lake Champlain from the upper end of Lake George, and thence by boat down the thirty-mile-long body of water to the small fort at its southern end. Time was short. There were rumors abroad that the British troops, assisted by Indians, might appear in force at any time from the Canadian end of Lake Champlain. Even should the regulars repossess the two forts, the munitions, at least, could be placed beyond their grasp.

There was a further reason for sending a force north to Lake Champlain—the defense of the entire province of New York, from the Quebec border all the way down to New York City, where the deputies were now sitting. The geography of this region made it so. The province had been settled along a chain of waterways which provided the most practical route for moving people and cargoes. The 100-mile extent of Lake Champlain, the 30 of Lake George, and the more than 160 miles of the Hudson River formed a strategic highway for an army. If it were not secured by the colonists of New York, the province and the city would be at the mercy of the enemy. The history of the recent war against the French had already demonstrated this lesson. Some of the most important battles and maneuvers had taken place in the upper New York region—a fact not lost on the Continental Congress.

After considering the implications of Allen and Arnold's raid on the shore of Lake Champlain, the Philadelphia Congress made its fears quite plain. It sent the New York Congress a message that declared:

"There is indubitable evidence that a design is formed by the British Ministry of making a cruel invasion from the Province of Quebec upon these Colonies, for the purpose of destroying our lives and liberties." The message went on to justify the taking of the forts by "inhabitants of the Northern Colonies" who were "impelled by a just regard for the defense and preservation of themselves and their countrymen from such imminent danger and calamities." The seized cannon and military stores, said the Continental Congress, "would certainly have been used in the intended invasion of these colonies." The New York Congress was asked to see to it that the stores were moved, and that a strong post to protect them was established at Lake George.

But the king's military property must be handled with responsibility, the Philadelphia Congress warned. The letter said that an exact record should be kept of all cannon and stores removed, "in order that they may be safely returned when the restoration of the former harmony between Great Britain and these colonies, so ardently wished for by the latter, shall render it prudent and consistent with the overruling law of self preservation."

This letter to New York from the Continental Congress breathed the air of defiance to the king's ministry. At the same time, it expressed the hope that beyond the musket-fire and bloodshed of this year would emerge a new "harmony" between Englishmen in America and their government overseas. Congress was thus shaking the clenched fist, while saying it was still willing to offer the open hand of friendship.

At the first meeting of the New York Congress which he attended, Richard Montgomery was appointed to a twelve-member committee to take charge of the captured arms and gunpowder. Few of his fellow committeemen had met Montgomery before he appeared in their midst as one of the deputies elected from Dutchess County, which lay fifty miles up the Hudson from New York City. But within a very short while the others recognized they were in the presence of a man of remarkable abilities for this work. Most members of the assembly had no experience whatsoever in organizing a force of troops and directing them in the transport of munitions. A few had been volunteer officers of the colonial militia, serving under the British army in the French and Indian War, fifteen years earlier. Since then, their military titles had become more honorary than meaningful, and they had hardly sniffed gunpowder except when firing a ceremonial cannon-salute. But to Richard Montgomery, a professional soldier for sixteen years, the task to which he was assigned was an old, familiar story. It is little wonder that he quickly emerged as the natural leader in military matters among this group of civilian merchants and lawyers.

When he first took his seat in the New York Congress, the Richard Montgomery whom the New York deputies met was a tall, moderately handsome gentleman of thirty-six, with a prominent brow, straight nose, and slightly receding chin. His eyes were blue, his smooth-shaven face already ruddy and somewhat tanned from the time he had spent outdoors in the winds and rain of the new season. His brown hair, unmarked by the white powder affected by some city dandies, was secured behind the neck by a short bow. Montgomery's physical appearance conveyed a sense of both grace and power, since his years as a soldier and later as a farmer permitted him no accumulation of excess flesh. Both in the saddle and on his feet, Montgomery held himself with the erect carriage of the aristocrat who felt pride in his social position and his education. Neatness of grooming and of dress was all of one piece with his straight-back posture.

This care for detail seemed an essential part of the man, for it carried over into Montgomery's choice of words, both in speech and in writing. He wrote in a clear, firm hand, and with a precision of expression that left no doubt of his meaning. He was not talkative like some of his colleagues; he deferred to the others when the discussion turned to theory and to politics. When he did speak on such exact matters as the weight of a cannon, or the number of men required to carry it to a boat, his manner of speaking was reserved. Indeed, it had a quality of understatement that lent his words greater force when the listener had absorbed them.

Exactly who, the deputies asked one another, is this earnest and able young man? Why has he revealed so much knowledge of the military problems of defending New York? Why has he, on his own initiative, surveyed the country north of the city? And why does he speak with such assurance of the points where defenses should be placed?

In those last days of May and into early June, as they conferred together, Richard Montgomery's colleagues drew from him, and from members of the old New York family into which he had married, some of the answers they sought.

Almost alone among the members of the Provincial Congress, Richard Montgomery was not an old New Yorker. He had settled in the province scarcely three years before, after having spent most of his previous years in the British Isles, and all his earlier adult life in the British army. A strange kind of background, indeed, for one who was taking the lead now in planning to defend New York against that same military force.

By birth Montgomery was Irish, not English. He was born on December 2, 1738 at the country seat of his father, Thomas Montgomery of County Donegal in Northern Ireland, not far from Dublin. The Montgomerys, however, were not Gaels of old Erin, being largely Anglo-Saxon in blood, and in faith thoroughly Church of England. The first Montgomery who settled in Donegal was among the soldiers rewarded at the end of the seventeenth century with estates granted by a grateful English King, William III, after his conquest of Ireland and the annexation of the northern counties to Great Britain. Thomas Montgomery, Richard's father, sat in the Parliament as a member for County Donegal, as did his eldest son, Alexander. Richard, his two elder brothers and his sister therefore grew up in a household of landed aristocracy, whose members were accustomed to govern and to lead. In their speech and their mode of life they stemmed from England and looked to her for their standards.

The Montgomerys were a proud family. Among the notables to whom they traced their lineage was Gabriel Montgomery, captain of the Scottish Guard of King Henry II of France, who when jousting with his monarch in 1559 had the ill fortune to cause his death by a wound in the eye. Later involved in a civil war against the throne, Montgomery was captured and executed. Among his descendants through several generations were noted military men, marked by their bravery and vigor. And so it was almost preordained that Richard, the youngest of the three men in his immediate family, and not eligible to inherit lands, should choose the king's military service as a career. Accordingly, after a liberal education at Trinity College in Dublin, he entered the British army as an ensign in 1756, when he was a few months short of his eighteenth birthday.

Montgomery's sixteen years in the service of King George II and King George III were all spent in one infantry regiment, the 17th Foot. Hardly had he become accustomed to his duties as the most junior of company officers when the 17th was posted to America, where France and Britain were locked in a bitter colonial struggle for mastery of the North American continent. The British colo-

nists in New York, Massachusetts and neighboring provinces termed it the "French and Indian War," identifying
the conflict by their opponents, who descended upon them
from the Province of Quebec and the wilderness to the northwest, between the St. Lawrence River settlements and those
close to the Atlantic Coast. In reality, however, the war was
far-flung, involving all the principal powers of Europe. It
was fought for seven years on the European Continent, on
the high seas and as far away as India.

Commissioned as the war was starting, Richard Montgomery quickly came of age in the army. From the outset he
found himself commanding men, some of whom were more
than twice his age, and making decisions governing their
welfare. The secure world of his boyhood, the County
Donegal manor and the classical college in Dublin, must
have quickly faded from his active consciousness. Thrust
into its place was his duty to take responsibility for others.
Not only was he charged with caring for the king's military
property, he also had to account for funds and disburse
them, as well as house, feed, equip, transport and inspect
the troops.

In this century of almost ceaseless warfare waged by professional soldiers, tight organization and severe discipline
had made the British army the most formidable fighting
force, unit for unit, in the world. The strength of the British
military system was based on the authority of its commanders. It was presumed that the soldier in the ranks, even
though he might be a man in his thirties or even forties,
was very much like a child. He had to be told what to do,
supervised at all times and punished when necessary. The
officers, in this scheme of things, were in the role of fathers
to the troops, and often called them "my boys." They were

expected to praise their charges when the "boys" performed
well, and even to reward certain of them with a few shillings
on occasion.

But when the troops misbehaved, and especially when
they disobeyed orders—the most grievous form of misbe-
havior—they were punished with severity. Floggings on the
bare back were common chastisements meted out to mis-
creant soldiers in the regiment as Richard Montgomery was
learning his officer's duties. And in an extreme case in wartime, a military execution for cowardice under fire, or for
desertion, served as a grim warning to all ranks when they
were turned out to witness a hanging while standing at attention.

In this tough, demanding school, Richard Montgomery
learned and made good. In 1758 he fought with the 17th
Foot at the siege and taking of Louisbourg, the strong
French fortress anchored solidly to the rocks of Cape Breton
Island. The capture of this obstacle to penetration of the St.
Lawrence River enabled the British fleet to move with security upstream toward the key city of French Canada, Quebec. Even as General James Wolfe prepared to close in on
Quebec, Montgomery's regiment was dispatched southwest
by sea. Its mission was to move with other troops under the
command of General Amherst through New York Province
by means of its close-linked waterways, and to strike at the
French from the the Hudson and Lake Champlain direction.

So it came about that in 1758 and 1759 Richard Montgomery, who had been promoted to the rank of lieutenant,
covered in General Amherst's campaign against the French
much of the territory that sixteen years later was to appear
to him again as a prospective battleground. In 1775, however, the looming struggle lay between the American colo-

nists and the British army. And, ironically, the British were in the geographical position that the French had occupied in the earlier war.

With the 17th Foot Regiment in the French and Indian War, Richard Montgomery mounted the Hudson Valley by boat and marched through much of upper New York Province. He was with the troops that occupied Lake George, Crown Point and Fort Ticonderoga, which the French had named Fort Carillon during the years when they had held it. He took part in months of reconnaissance and maneuvering by small scouting parties in the thick, forested mountain country, as the British probed for signs of a French attack that never came.

In September of 1759, when General Wolfe finally closed in on Quebec City and prepared to assault this critical point in the defense system of French Canada, Montgomery's regiment was at Albany, on the upper Hudson. General Amherst responded to Wolfe's call for support, and force-marched his men at a terrible pace northward to the long lakes, in the hope of reaching the scene of action in time. But as the troops under Amherst hastened down the length of Lake Champlain, and followed the swift Sorel River * that flows from that lake north to the St. Lawrence River, news arrived of the glorious British victory on the Plains of Abraham, just outside the walls of Quebec. Wolfe and his opponent, the courtly and distinguished General Montcalm, had both been killed in the battle. But the British flag now flew proudly over the principal city of Canada, and Montcalm's once formidable army had been smashed. There remained but little opposition to the British redcoats, to be mopped up at will during the coming spring campaign.

* The Sorel River is named the Richelieu River on modern maps.

With the Canadian phase of the war virtually over, the 17th was sent to the West Indies. By this time Montgomery's intelligence and devotion to his duties had attracted the attention of the regimental commander. Colonel Monckton, who in New York had served in the twin roles of soldier and governor of the province, appointed Montgomery as his regimental adjutant. For a young officer of twenty-one, this was a promising sign that he might be on his way up the ladder of military promotion.

In the Caribbean theater of action, Richard Montgomery took part in further fighting against the French, and was present at the capture of Martinique, off the coast of South America, and of Havana, on the island of Cuba. Here he suffered from the semitropical heat and fevers to the same degree that just a year or two before he had been half frozen by the cold winds and snow in the mountain country of upper New York and Canada. With the end of the war in 1763 he returned to England with his regiment in the rank of captain, a six-year veteran now commanding his own company at age twenty-four.

Peacetime army life appealed then, as it sometimes does now, to the unimaginative and not exceedingly ambitious officer. But to one of Montgomery's restless temperament these were dull years, full of parade-ground pomp and barracks boredom, while time and promotions moved at the pace of a snail. Montgomery employed his leisure hours reading deeply in history, the classics, and the various practical sciences which came under the heading of "natural philosophy." He likewise took a keen interest in observing the political struggles between the liberal Whigs, who looked to such men as Burke, Fox and Barré for inspiration, and the Conservative faction, or Tories, grouped around Grenville, Townshend and Lord North. Here, Montgomery must have recognized, in the world of political ideals and philosophies, was a battleground as important as that of cannon and musket-fire. There were fortresses to storm and heights to be taken in other fields than those of the war god, Mars, if one had the tenacity and the intelligence to work to those ends.

The critical point in Richard Montgomery's army career came in 1772, nine years after his last genuine military action. Now he was thirty-three years old, and still just a captain in the 17th Foot. He was bored with the army routine, and intrigued by his reading and discussions of public affairs with the thought of looking for something else to do. Then a major's commission in the regiment fell vacant. Montgomery posted the necessary money to "buy the majority," according to the prevailing custom of promotion in the upper ranks of the British army. But his hopes were dashed when another man was appointed in his stead. Now it appeared certain that in the army he was destined to rust in idleness, dressed and equipped for heroic deeds but with no chance to perform them. Thoroughly disillusioned with the military as a career, Montgomery resigned his commission and decided to cross the Atlantic to America, buy a good piece of property, and became a gentleman farmer. In that way he could be putting his energies to constructive use.

During his wartime service in New York, Montgomery had been impressed with the richness of the country and the almost limitless opportunities it offered a man of spirit and energy. He had visited some colonists in their homes and from them had learned that with enough capital to get started on his own farm, a gentleman could build it into a productive estate. The land in Britain was crowded. Because elder sons, like his brother Alexander Montgomery, by custom inherited the father's lands, younger sons like himself were surplus in country manors. In America, however, an enterprising gentleman could buy land easily, and he could hire any number of immigrant workmen who were pouring into the port towns on almost every ship from the British Isles. With the labor of indentured tenants he could build a fine house and outbuildings, clear fields and raise livestock by the time his hired men had completed their required period of service.

Montgomery had seen that the New York colonists lived well. Their newly built estates that lined the shores of the Hudson River, and many of the fine houses that dotted the rolling surface of York Island and other places near the town of New York, were as well equipped and as comfortable as many country homes in England and Northern Ireland. Wood for the hearth and for building grew without limit in the colony. In contrast, the British Isles had for a long time lacked sufficient timber. In New York Province there was clay for making brick, stone in profusion awaiting the quarryman's hammer, ores for the ironmaker, and land —empty land stretching as far as the eye could see.

Late in 1772, Richard Montgomery reached New York and purchased a farm about a mile north of King's Bridge, near a point where the creek which the Indians had named Mosholu bordered the old Dutch community of Yonkers on the west side, and the English settlement to the east called Fordham. It was a favorable spot for orchards and grazing, close to the conjunction of the Albany and Boston post roads, with the navigable waters of Harlem Creek flowing nearby. By boat or by road, the city of New York lay a scant twelve or thirteen miles to the southward.

Within a short time of his taking up the life of a New

York farmer, Richard Montgomery was touched on the shoulder by the hand of destiny. Perhaps it happened when he visited New York City to make purchases from the first cargoes of the spring shipping season to arrive from England. Whenever, or however, it occurred, Montgomery again met Janet Livingston after an interval of fourteen years. He had seen her first during the late war when he was an ambitious lieutenant of the 17th Foot, only twenty years old, and with no expectation other than to make a career in the army. At the time Janet was a girl of sixteen, the eldest child in the large family of Judge Robert R. Livingston, the squire of Clermont. En route up the Hudson Valley by boat, the 17th had come ashore near the Livingston estate, which lay some seventy miles upstream from New York City. Several of the officers, including Montgomery, had accepted the hospitality offered there by Judge and Mrs. Livingston and their daughter Janet.

The first meeting had amounted to little more than the typically hurried wartime acquaintance, that occurs over and over again between soldier and girl wherever armies march. They met and parted within one day. But this time there was no hurrying away at duty's call. Richard Montgomery was settling in New York to stay, a gentleman without a family on the American side of a vast ocean. And Janet, now close to thirty, was still Miss Livingston. She was graceful, attractive and accomplished—the kind of lady to intrigue a bachelor of Montgomery's stripe, who had but recently doffed the king's uniform to become the proprietor of his own land. In the springtime he courted her, in May he had won her consent, and forthwith Richard Montgomery was writing a suitor's respectful letter to Judge Livingston asking his daughter's hand in marriage.

The Livingstons were a notable family in the colony, prosperous and highly educated. Judge Livingston of the Supreme Court of the Province of New York was not one to deal lightly with the welfare of his daughter, so he required some time before he gave his answer. The Judge's grandfather had come to America from Scotland a full century before, and himself married into one of the most prosperous of the Dutch families, the Van Rensselaers, and had risen quickly to a position of wealth and influence through successful trade with the Indians. He obtained a royal patent to form a huge estate, Livingston Manor, which spread along the Hudson to the extent of 160,000 acres. Since that time his descendants had generous space on which to build their own homes, to raise crops and livestock, and to lease or sell parcels of land profitably to later arrivals in the colony. A leader in the Whig party in New York, Judge Livingston had been a judge of the admiralty court in the city, and for the past ten years had served as judge of the Supreme Court of the colony.

It is possible that Richard Montgomery's background in the British army may have given the Judge pause, for he was an ardent patriot leader. The army personified the repressive acts of the Tory ministers in England, and the bright red uniform was not a pleasant sight in New York now, as it had been during the French and Indian War. Livingston had been a delegate to the 1766 Stamp Act Congress that had protested successfully against the imposition of the stamp tax. More recently he had been chairman of the New York Committee of Correspondence, part of the intelligence network that kept the dissenters of thirteen colonies in touch with one another, from New Hampshire to Georgia.

A military officer beholden to the ministry and the crown for advancement was not likely to think well of the political outlook of the Judge and his friends, and the feelings would be mutual. But Montgomery's resignation from the army was in his favor, and doubtless the admiration he expressed for the Whig leaders in Parliament—Burke, Fox, and others who sided with the colonies—must have stood well with Judge Livingston. For in June the older man replied to the suitor that he had "made such enquiries as have given a great deal of satisfaction" in regard to Montgomery as a prospective son-in-law. Accordingly, in July 1773, Richard Montgomery and Janet Livingston were married in Clermont, in the presence of a large company of Livingston relatives and friends.

As the husband of Judge Livingston's daughter, Montgomery literally acquired a large family all at once, a clan that pulled him into its circle of intimacy and its way of life. He leased his farm at King's Bridge and moved up the Hudson to the Livingston domain, where Janet owned property on the east bank of the river not far from the village of Rhinebeck. As if he were striving to make up for all the years he had missed while wandering across the world as a soldier, then waiting in vain for promotion, Montgomery set vigorously to work. A house of brick and wood was built, fields were plowed, pastureland was fenced, and the Montgomery farm was on its way to becoming a prosperous enterprise as well as a comfortable country seat. The first tasks out of the way, Montgomery started to build a grain mill, there being a ready supply of water on his land to turn the millwheels.

But it was not all work for the soldier turned farmer, because the indoors months of winter gave the Livingstons of

Dutchess County and their friends time to visit and to exchange ideas. Clermont, the largest, most tastefully furnished of the mansions in the area, was a favorite gathering place and a center of hospitality, with its large main hall leading to a staircase of grand design, and its imported mahogany doors set in delicately carved framework. In such a gracious house it was a pleasure to visit, to dine and to talk. And the sparks flew in profusion during the heated discussions before the warm fireplaces of Clermont, for the house of Judge Livingston was a hotbed of informed, articulate colonialist discontent.

Here at Clermont, as in neighboring houses around Rhinebeck, Richard Montgomery during the first two years of his marriage was shown the iniquity of the British colonial system. He had seen some of the rot of corruption in the army—the cheating and pilfering, the shoddy supplies for which the Treasury paid good gold, the scrambling for favor and position. Now he was hearing from the people bearing the burden of the system.

His informants were not ignorant malcontents of the lower class. These new neighbors of his, and his relatives by marriage, were men of intelligence and education, reading and thinking men, some of whom had studied at Yale College in New Haven, and at King's College in New York. The Judge, to be sure, was the leading spirit among the patriots in this county. But not far behind him in learning, and perhaps ahead in his keenness of intellect, was his eldest son. A lawyer like his father, trained at King's College, the younger Robert R. Livingston was only twenty-six when Montgomery moved into the bosom of the family. Despite the eight years difference in their ages, the two became fast friends almost from the start, attracted to one another by the bond of intellectual companionship as strong as the family tie that had made them brothers-in-law.

In long hours of talk with Robert, by the fire in foul weather, and on the hunt in fair, Montgomery found his eyes opened to the injustices of ministerial rule that had aroused the rage of the colonists. For now that he was working with all his energies and with his own hands to create wealth in this productive land, he felt as one with the Livingstons and their friends who had done the same for generations.

Taxes to pay for defense of the British Empire against the French were quite understandable—but the French were no longer a menace to these colonies. The Indians? A few military outposts to the north and west garrisoned by a handful of men with muskets would keep the savages where they belonged. It was quite acceptable to pay taxes, of course, to support the king's courts, and even to provide the royal governor with his salary, his horses and carriages, and his clerks.

But taxation of these earnest, hard-working gentlemen of America, to pay for the lavish spending of a corrupt government in London, to which the taxed were not even privileged to send representatives—this now appeared to Montgomery a shocking injustice. The governed, as the Livingstons argued, should have a share in their own government. The taxed should determine their taxes. Parliament must listen to the colonies. If not, all the soldiers and all the men-of-war that the ministry might send could not make them bend their knee willingly to despotism.

As he was absorbing the viewpoint of the colonial resistants to ministerial policy, Richard Montgomery was also revealing to Robert and to the Judge, perhaps without knowing it, a considerable amount of himself. Through the better part of two years, as this new member of their family was drawn closer to them in affection and in political attitudes, the Livingstons realized that Richard Montgomery was an asset of prime value to the colonial cause. A professional soldier who knew the British army as thoroughly as anyone of his age could know it, this young man was a logical candidate for leadership—if their resistance should ever come to war. The Livingstons thought more deeply than most men about them, and therefore saw the future with greater clarity. They realized that while hoping for peace, the American colonies must secretly prepare to fight for the liberties they held dear.

It was therefore no accident that when the New York leaders met early in 1775 to choose delegates to the Second Continental Congress at Philadelphia, Robert R. Livingston, only twenty-eight years of age, was one of those selected. And when a meeting was held at Rhinebeck on May 16th to name the Dutchess County deputies to the Provincial Congress, Richard Montgomery was one of the ten men designated. Intensely interested in political developments, though not an active seeker after any place or office, he reluctantly consented to the assignment. After spending the better part of a week managing to put affairs in order at his farm, Montgomery set off for New York City. Riding a hard eighty miles, he reached the Exchange in time to hear the decision to remove the cannon, shot and gunpowder from Fort Ticonderoga. Then, within the day, he found himself a member of the committee appointed to carry out the plan.

Meanwhile, in Philadelphia, the Continental Congress was step by step behaving more like an active government than merely a conference. At each day's meeting, the clerk who kept the journal wrote soberly that "the Congress met and resolved itself into a committee of the whole to take into consideration the state of America." Each day's "consideration" resulted in certain specific actions, or decisions that a small working committee was appointed to execute. Thus, the Continental Congress acted as both legislature and executive, impelled by the growing conviction on the part of all delegates that they must present a united front if they were to find salvation from tyranny.

On May 17th, the Continental Congress resolved unanimously that all exports to Quebec and the islands of Canada should immediately cease. Furthermore, no provisions of any kind should be furnished the British merchantmen on the American coasts, for fear they might supply the British army and fleet. On the 19th, a committee appointed to consider what military posts should be occupied in the colony of New York, and the number of troops needed to guard them, was brought in and discussed behind closed doors for the next week. By the twenty-seventh, the Congress had determined to send an appeal to the inhabitants of Canada, asking their support and understanding should warfare break out near the Quebec-New York border. On the same day, the Congress appointed George Washington of Virginia and five other men to a committee to plan ways and means of supplying the united colonies with arms and ammunition, and to report immediately.

On May 29th, five days after Richard Montgomery had ridden into New York City, a message which struck directly home reached the Exchange. John Hancock, president of the Continental Congress, urged that the New York leaders move swiftly and secretly to plan the defense of New York City and Province against a blow that the Congress believed was imminent. The Congress had resolved, first, that a post be immediately fortified at or near King's Bridge, urging "that the ground be chosen with a particular view to prevent the communication between the city of New York and the country from being interrupted by land."

Montgomery, without doubt, could already visualize the site of the best possible defense posts in his mind's eye: a hill on his own farm just north of Manhattan Island, that looked down on King's Bridge and the junction of the Albany and Boston post roads; the high point above the Blue Bell tavern, that dominated the island's main road for more than two miles; a couple of lesser heights at intervals of a half mile northward on the same spiny ridge near the Hudson cliffs; and possibly an abrupt height a half mile east of the Blue Bell, from which good cannon, well manned, could cover the Harlem River for a mile or more below Dyckman's Bridge.

Instructions from the Continental Congress continued to spell out preparations for war in this theater. In the Highlands of the Hudson, several parallel ranges of mountains came down sharply to the water's edge, and compressed the river into a narrow S-curve at a place called West Point. Here the Congress counseled New York to mount artillery batteries, to prevent the passage of any hostile ships of war "that may be sent to harass the inhabitants on the border of said river." Experienced persons should be sent at once to examine the terrain and decide on the point where shipping could be obstructed to the defenders' best advantage.

Further, said the Congress, the militia of New York should be armed, and training should start at once. A force of men should be held in readiness within the city to protect the inhabitants "in case any insult should be offered by the troops that may land there, and to prevent any attempts that may be made to gain possession of the city." New York itself should decide the number of men required, up to a maximum of three thousand, and should appoint the necessary officers. The Congress recommended, in view of the lack of money, that the province not pay an enlistment bounty to the men, nor issue them clothing, and the province should pay them no more than the nominal pay fixed by the New England colonies for their volunteers. Unless the Continental Congress should direct them to disband sooner, the troops should be enlisted to serve only through the last day of December.

Finally, the resolution from Philadelphia urged New York, defense preparations should be pushed vigorously because the Congress "is very uncertain whether the earnest endeavors of the Congress to accommodate the unhappy differences between Great Britain and the Colonies, by conciliatory measures, will be successful."

Now the New York deputies saw war staring them directly in the face. They moved quickly. On the same day that these instructions from Philadelphia reached the city, the assembly at the Exchange took action on several fronts. A quick message was sent to the New Jersey Provincial Congress stating that New York was ready and anxious to confer on matters of mutual concern. Between the lines, this meant defense of the lower Hudson River, which could be controlled for twenty miles from the tableland above the towering cliffs on the New Jersey side, which were even more formidable than the steep banks of upper Manhattan Island.

A dispatch went back to the New York contingent in Philadelphia complaining that "there is no powder to be purchased in this city, and scarce any in the whole colony." Furthermore, a considerable number of the inhabitants are without arms, Congress was told. Messages from Governor Trumbull of Connecticut and from Benedict Arnold at Crown Point were read, then forwarded to the Continental Congress. Montgomery's committee charged with the removal of stores from Ticonderoga was ordered to send to the fort, "as privately as possible," one hundred barrels of pork, two hundred barrels of flour, and twenty barrels of rum. These were provisions to prepare for a long defense—if need be, through the coming winter.

Now Richard Montgomery was recognized as the indispensable man. On May 30th, beyond his other duties, he was named to a five-member committee to carry out the instructions of Congress to prepare to defend upper Manhattan. The group's orders were "to view the ground at or near King's Bridge and report to this Congress whether the ground near King's Bridge shall admit of making a fortification that will be tenable; and at what particular place the ground will admit of making the best and most tenable fortification."

As he rode out of town with Gouverneur Morris and the other committee members to survey the site, Montgomery must have taken a gloomy view of the prospect. In his eyes, this ground was not tenable at all, should the British enter New York in strength. But how could he tell his colleagues that their city could probably not be defended successfully? He recognized that these were men of fighting spirit, whose hearts beat with a passionate desire for liberty, and who were apparently willing to take up musket and sword to fight for their rights. And yet, in the business of fighting a

war, they were virtually all untried amateurs, without training to lead soldiers or plan a campaign.

God only knew where New York would find the men to
follow them against a disciplined body of British regulars,
should it come to open warfare!

o.

3

Continental Brigadier

A s THE New York Congress prepared actively to defend the city and the Hudson Valley, an express rider reached Philadelphia carrying an ominous dispatch from Lake Champlain. Benedict Arnold wrote that four hundred British regulars had assembled dangerously close to his post at Crown Point, and threatened to attack. Men who had passed that way told Arnold that the troops were busily preparing a flotilla of flat-bottomed gunboats at Fort St. John's, on the Sorel River, a few miles from the northern end of the lake.

St. John's was a strongpoint composed of two fortifications, roughly rectangular in shape. These were built of heavy earth and log breastworks, and were situated two hundred yards apart, with connecting trenches. The fort was so positioned that it protected a work space along the west bank where large armed gunboats could be built and launched on the Sorel. The fort itself controlled all traffic on the river, as well as that on the north-south road which led to the town of Sorel, where the swift-flowing river of that name emptied into the broad St. Lawrence. Backing St. John's as a source of men and supplies was Montreal, the large town on the St. Lawrence just one day's march to the northwest.

In the American direction, St. John's was protected by another soundly built fort at the Ile aux Noix, or "Nut Island." This wooded island lay about twenty miles upstream from St. John's, close to the surveyor's line that separated New York Province from Quebec. Here the waterway was so narrow on both sides of the island, and the terrain so open, that a few guns at the fort could prevent any craft from passing from Lake Champlain downstream toward St. John's.

The message from Arnold reflected his fear of imminent danger. He asserted that the British regulars were preparing to move down the lake at any moment, and "expected to be joined by a number of Indians, with a design of retaking Crown Point and Ticonderoga." Arnold appealed earnestly for reinforcements and supplies, clearly showing that he considered his present force too weak to hold out against a serious attack.

One important fact that Arnold did not state openly, but that Congress had heard from various sources during the past few weeks, was that Benedict Arnold and Ethan Allen had been at each other's throats in a jealous rivalry for leadership. Each of these two men styled himself a "colonel," and they both resented the other's presence as a shadow cast on his own glory. Both were ambitious, brave and daring— and at the same time highly irresponsible. There was no telling at what point either of them, if supplied with sufficient men and arms, might take it into his head to attack the Ile aux Noix, or even St. John's, on his own. Neither was the type to await the orders, or even to ask permission, of his provincial congress or of the Continental Congress. So it was not certain in Philadelphia whether Arnold was genuinely asking help to defend his position. He might be planning to conduct his own offensive into Canada, once he should get the men and munitions he sought.

Arnold and Allen had managed to reach a temporary settlement of their quarrel by putting a dozen miles between them. Allen and his Green Mountain Boys held Fort Ticonderoga, while Arnold, with a scattering of men from Connecticut, New Hampshire and New York, stayed at Crown Point, a short march to the north. If the British should strike down the lake in strength, Arnold's position lay exposed first. The Crown Point defense works were light, and lay right on the lake shore. A concentrated attack from gunboats on the lake and from one or two hundred men landing on either flank could overwhelm him.

Ticonderoga, on the other hand, was built on a height that was fairly easy to defend on three sides, if it were sufficiently garrisoned. In the last war, the French under General Montcalm had beaten back a British attacking force here with heavy losses. And at the moment Fort Ticonderoga held the bulk of the captured British cannon, shot and gunpowder.

It was a delicate situation, posing questions that Congress found difficult to answer at such a distance. How much of the stores should be moved away from Ticonderoga to secure them from capture? How much should be left to defend the two lake forts? Uncertain about making a decision on military tactics, Congress threw the problem to the two provincial governments closer at hand. A hasty message to Governor Trumbull of Connecticut proposed that he send a strong reinforcement to the Champlain posts, and that as much of the stores be kept there as were needed to hold them. The New York Congress, in turn, was asked to send food and equipment to the troops at Lake Champlain as quickly as possible. Most important, Congress told Governor Trumbull that he should appoint an officer in whom he had full confidence to take over command of both points.

Yet as long as Arnold and Allen should remain near the frontier, danger hovered thick over the lake country. The crucial point was to avoid any act that would turn the inhabitants of Quebec Province against the thirteen united colonies. The province of Quebec, largely inhabited by French-speaking colonists, had not yet been digested by the British Empire in the few years since its conquest. The people were just beginning to get used to government from England, a strange, new idea to them, and only within the past year had been brought under a new governing law, the Quebec Act. Although a few individual Canadians were known to be sympathetic to the cause of the united colonies, Canadians generally had not taken part in the resistance of the past few years. The province of Quebec had no delegates in Philadelphia. In case of war, the Continental Congress could not tell where the sympathies of most Canadians would lie.

For this reason, the border region was no place in which to permit two firebrands like Benedict Arnold and Ethan Allen complete freedom of action. One act of violence, even though committed in the name of liberty, might cost America a terrible price. Congress was therefore concerned that no latitude be given to anyone to conduct a raid across the border. If the united colonies were to offend the Canadians, and turn them against the cause of American liberty, the British military would be the gainers. But if, on the other hand, the people of Quebec could be won over, and would join the resistance movement, then the British army and fleet would not enjoy a secure base in Canada from which to attack Massachusetts, Connecticut and New York.

Accordingly, the day after it considered Arnold's plea for reinforcements, the Congress solemnly passed a resolution declaring that:

> "As this Congress has nothing more in view than the defense of these colonies, Resolved that no expedition or intrusion ought to be undertaken or made by any colony, or body of colonists, against or into Canada."

Congress saw to it that this decision was at once dispatched to Arnold and Allen, as well as to New York and the other colonies bordering on Canada. It was ordered further that the resolution be translated into French and distributed, by whatever means possible, among the inhabitants of Canada. A day later, on June 2nd, the New York Congress sought on its own to reassure the inhabitants of Quebec of their friendship, and to beg them to resist attempts by "enemies of our King and his people" to excite "jealousies and discord amongst us."

The New York Assembly's open letter to the Canadians said: "We consider you as our friends, and we feel for you the affection of brothers." It went on to explain that, "Ministerial tyranny hath endeavored, throughout all these colonies, to rend from us the dearest rights of humanity; and in the defense of those rights some persons have taken certain forts in this Colony, which are near your frontiers. . . .

Our only intention is to prevent any hostile incursions upon us by the troops of your Province."

Even as these reassurances were being sent to the Canadians, the leaders of the united colonies were planning night and day for the clash at arms they felt sure was coming. On June 3rd Richard Montgomery found time to write a letter to his brother-in-law, Robert R. Livingston, who since the middle of May had been in Philadelphia as a member of the delegation from New York. As they did frequently, the two men exchanged views frankly, because each knew the mind of the other. Montgomery explained to Livingston that he could not understand why the Continental Congress had decided to erect defense posts near King's Bridge. Even if the New Yorkers did hold the bridge, Montgomery wrote, communication between the mainland and upper Manhattan could be interrupted "by posts occupied by an enemy near the Blue Bell," or other points nearby.

Of course, Montgomery's analysis went on, if an enemy should land on the island, we would try to confine them to as small an area as possible. To do this our troops would have to fight on Manhattan Island itself, and free communication with the country to the north would be necessary. However, he wrote, the necessary defense posts can be constructed quickly, and "will be best effected by the troops.

"If we make those works before we have troops, we may make them for somebody else."

In other terms, should the colonists build strongpoints above the city before they had the men and arms to defend them, British soldiers might quickly use them to isolate the town of New York from the rest of the province.

A first-rate, practical engineer to take charge of fortification planning is what New York most requires right now, Montgomery wrote to Livingston. "Inquire among your friends in Philadelphia. I only know enough to be afraid of undertaking what I never had any practice in, and would much rather examine the plans of others than give one of my own."

Then, turning to the political situation, Montgomery assured Robert of his hearty wish that attempts at accommodation with Britain might succeed. Indeed, the former British officer said he himself had high hopes that the colonies would reach an accord with the mother country. Yet, he continued, we must be constantly on guard against treachery. He relayed to Robert his suspicions that a certain scheming gentleman was laying plans to garrison Fort Ticonderoga with New York troops under the influence of Tory leaders, and then to give it up to General Guy Carleton, the British commander in Canada.

As to the matter of selecting military leaders for the united colonies, Montgomery was well aware that his own name was under consideration. Robert wanted to know Montgomery's thoughts on possible commanders. What of Philip Schuyler, a member of the New York delegation in Philadelphia, one of the richest and most prominent landowners in New York? Schuyler, now forty-two, had been a colonel of New York militia in the war against the French. A man of power and influence, he was a leading figure in the patriotic movement. What did Montgomery think of him as a leader of New York troops?—Robert wanted to know.

"His consequence in the province makes him a fit subject for an important trust," the professional soldier replied. "But has he *strong nerves*?" Montgomery underlined the words expressing the cardinal point on which Schuyler's ability to command should be judged. Past service and prominence were useful, of course, in choosing leaders. But, Montgomery asked his brother-in-law, who was in a position to probe more deeply into Schuyler's character, what of his courage to make the hard decisions, and to stand up under the consequences?

"I would wish to have that point well ascertained with respect to any man so employed," Montgomery concluded.

In this busy springtime of preparation for war, the demands for action knocked so loudly on the door that there was no time for relaxed thought over every decision. On June 6th the New York Congress called in Henry Watkeys, a gunsmith of the town, and questioned him briefly on his readiness to turn out gun barrels and muskets in large quantity for New York troops. Watkeys could not handle the order alone; but with a partner he might. By afternoon he was riding north on the Boston Post Road on his way to New Windsor, Connecticut, to work out a manufacturing agreement with an armorer named Robert Boyd in that town.

The clerk then read a letter from the New York members of the Continental Congress asking for the names of two men to whom "a warm recommendation" could be given as generals of the Continental Army. The first commander would hold the rank of Major General and the second would become a Brigadier General. The New York body was asked to submit the nominations as rapidly as possible, and to give reasons for their selections. A debate followed, without decision, and the choice was postponed until the following morning.

Early on June 7th before the congress met, Montgomery was again writing to Robert Livingston. New York's supply of gunpowder was much on his mind, as well as the command for which a number of the deputies were promoting him. Although he must have been heavily wearied and short of time, he took the occasion to jest about a powder-maker who was supposed to have reported for work long before this. He had "heard nothing" from the man, Montgomery told Robert, adding: "I hope he is not blown up."

About eight hundredweight of powder had been brought into the city the other night, Montgomery continued, and he believed there would be more, though he could not depend on its reaching New York soon. He said it should be very sparingly used:

> "Ammunition is an essential point. For my own part, should I have any command, I should use it with more scarcity than has been usual of late years in military operations."

Then turning to his own position as a prospective military leader:

> "I would most willingly decline any military command from a consciousness of want of talents. Nevertheless I shall sacrifice my own inclinations to the service of the public, if our Congress should be of the opinion they cannot find a more capable public servant."

Overnight there must have been considerable persuasive talking to various deputies on the part of John Morin Scott of New York City, and Gouverneur Morris of Westchester County. Both men had served on the military planning committees with Richard Montgomery, and by this time they must have been well acquainted with the depth of his professional knowledge and the soundness of his judgment. For when the nomination of officers was brought up the congress, as the clerk noted the event in his minute-book,

> ". . . unanimously resolved and agreed that Colonel Philip Schuyler is the most proper person in this Colony to be recommended as a Major General, and Richard Montgomery, Esq., as a Brigadier General;
>
> "And ordered, that Mr. Scott and Mr. Morris be a committee to prepare and report the draft of a letter to our delegates at the Continental Congress, informing them of our sentiments on this subject, and the reasons for our choice."

On the day that Montgomery was nominated for second-in-command for New York, there was much other business to transact, and the New York Congress lost no time getting to it. Gouverneur Morris reported that the committee sent out to examine the ground for fortifications near King's Bridge had concluded that it was unwise to build forts until New York had the troops and arms to secure them. Richard Montgomery's tactical ideas, which he had expressed privately to Robert, ran through the committee report and Morris's explanation of it. When a body of trained troops were on foot, but not before, Morris stated, a post capable of containing three hundred men should be built, at a spot designated "A" on the accompanying map. The assembly voted its approval of the report, then turned at once to pressing business—speeding stores and men to Fort Ticonderoga.

Artillerymen and gunsmiths were the men most needed in the north. Without them, the garrison could not prepare the captured weapons for use. As to building materials, stone and logs with which to strengthen the forts would have to be found nearby. New York could supply fifty spades and hoes, and dispatched a pair of expert masons. But even if all repairs were made in time, Ticonderoga and Crown Point could not be fully protected if the forces there merely sat still and awaited an attack. The Americans would have to prepare to fight the British on the lake itself, and should attempt to destroy their vessels before they landed troops in strength. Accordingly, the congress voted to send twelve ship's carpenters, if they could be persuaded to go, and a supply of hatchets, broadaxes, rope of various thicknesses, twine, sewing palms, sail needles, hoisting equipment, hammers and other tools.

The British had a long supply line behind their river and lake craft, reaching back to the many towns along the Sorel and St. Lawrence. But the New Yorkers were forced to build whatever craft they were to have in the open meadows and woodlands flanking the lake. In that sparsely settled part of the province, there were few shops with the equipment to build boats, and little in the way of materials for them to use. Yet already the blows of the broadaxes were ringing out in the Adirondack mountain country as the Green Mountain Boys set about hewing timbers to build a lake fleet as best they could. No time to season the green wood, with the enemy likely to appear any day on the blue lake stretching north from the forts so lightly held. Logs with the spring sap running within them would have to do. And, fortunately, there were a few men scattered hereabouts who had helped the British army build sailing sloops and flat-bottomed row-galleys on this same lake shore during the war with the French, in 1758. Their art was not completely lost, although it had slept for long years.

The need for cool heads in command at Champlain was made quite plain the day after Montgomery was nominated as a Continental Brigadier. A rambling letter from Ethan Allen reached the Congress. Apparently drunk with the ease of his military success so far, Allen openly advocated that he lead an invasion of Canada! If the New York deputies would only supply him with a few hundred men and sufficient artillery supplies, he would take Montreal, sweep through the entire province of Quebec, and push the British into the sea. The grandiose language of his message sounded like a tipsy tavern-orator trying to overwhelm his listeners with the color of his words.

Lake Champlain, Allen declared, is the key both to Canada and to New York, as well as her neighboring colonies. Everything depends on which military force should hold it. This key, he wrote,

". . . is ours as yet, and provided the Colonies would suddenly push an army of two or three thousand men into Canada, they might make a conquest of all that would oppose them. . . .

"I wish to God that America would, at this critical juncture, exert herself agreeable to the indignity offered her by a tyrannical Ministry. She might rise on eagles' wings, and mount up to glory, freedom and immortal honor, if she did but know and exert her strength. Fame is now hovering over her head. . . .

"I will stake my life on it, that with fifteen hundred men and a proper train of artillery, I will take Montreal."

Allen went on to declare that there were but seven hundred regular British troops in Canada. The French-speaking "habitants," as they were called, were at heart friendly to the American cause, but would not act against the redcoats on their own. The Indians, Allen said, would side with the more powerful force, and would join the colonists against the British as soon as the Americans got the upper hand in their country.

But if the New York Congress should think it "premature and imprudent" to push an army into Canada, Ethan Allen proposed as a substitute plan that he at least be empowered to occupy the Ile aux Noix. The advantage in doing so, he declared, would be to bottle up the British craft within the Sorel River. This alone, he said, might protect Lake Champlain, and prevent its being turned into a military highway for the British to penetrate New York.

Hardly had Allen's bold proposal been read out in New York than Connecticut received a similar boast from Benedict Arnold. He, too, declared that he could "take Canada" with just a few hundred sturdy men and a train of supplies. Both adventurous would-be invaders of Quebec quickly received firm instructions from Philadelphia and from the provincial governments: they were to undertake no more "private ventures" like the one that had put them in their present delicate position on Lake Champlain.

The time had obviously come for Congress to establish a Continental Army under a unified command. Discipline and organization had become essential. Guerrilla actions were no longer suitable. Fine weather had arrived, and any day now might see a large fleet of armed British ships loaded with troops arriving in the port towns of the North American coast. The Continental Congress and the provincial congresses were now desperately working to prepare, on a scale few men had conceived just three months before.

By June 9th, Richard Montgomery was busy on another committee, this one planning ways to supply a force of three thousand New York men and officers. Every article that might be needed in the field was put down. Simultaneously every shop and warehouse was scoured, room by room, shelf by shelf, to see what was at hand that could be used. Messengers rode out to other towns to secure what they could, and the rest would have to be obtained by hasty manufacture in homes and workshops. Muskets, carrying straps, knapsacks, blankets, powder horns, water bottles, cooking pots, horses, wagons, harness, tents, rope, hatchets —the list of items wanting seemed endless.

The army could not come into being unless it were to have equipment that made it an army, rather than a band of armed individuals. After all tribute was paid to their bravery, the Massachusetts men who had fired on the British regulars in April along the Boston-Concord road were not an army, or any part of one. They were a group of partisans, and little more. Each man shot his musket from the protection of a stone wall or tree, then ran away as he pleased. The Lexington and Concord farmers had no organization, and no equipment other than what each of them chose to bring with him that day. The city of New York and the Hudson Valley could not be protected in that irregular fashion. New York must have an organized army, properly equipped and led by officers with a battle plan.

By June 13th, the New York Congress had appointed Montgomery to a committee of three members authorized to supply the colony with one thousand good muskets. Henry Watkeys, the New York gunsmith, and Robert Boyd of Connecticut, by pooling their efforts and hiring a greatly increased force of laborers, assured the congress that they could turn out the thousand muskets, lock, stock and barrel, complete with steel ramrods, bayonets and scabbards, at a price of three pounds, fifteen shillings in New York money for each good set.

While the process of bringing the colony to arms was under way, it was in Philadelphia that the Continental army was being organized. On June 15th the Continental Congress unanimously chose George Washington of Virginia as General and Commander in Chief of the armed forces being raised by the united colonies. Within the week that followed, Congress chose four major generals, Philip Schuyler of New York among them. It named Horatio Gates of Virginia as Adjutant General, and on June 22nd completed the roster of generals by naming eight brigadiers. Second in rank among the eight was Richard Montgomery.

Since the seat of open fighting so far had largely been in New England, most of the newly named generals were New Englanders. But among the fourteen men in whom the Continental Congress entrusted the leadership of the united colonies in arms, Montgomery, Gates and Major General Charles Lee of Virginia were virtually the only ones who had experience as professional British soldiers. As part of their common background these three men had fought the French in America, had become deeply attached to the country, had quit the British military service and settled in the colonies in recent years. Gates, at forty-eight, was the eldest. Lee, who was drawing a retirement pension, was forty-four, nearly eight years the senior of Montgomery.

But the rest of the generals designated by Congress, including Washington himself, had been officers of the colonial militia rather than professionals. They were strong leaders, men of influence and initiative in their own provinces, who had displayed their patriotic colors long ago. But they would have to learn how to command an army, and learn quickly. Their practice of military art had not been kept shiny through years of use.

Acting under the impending shadow of attack from overseas, the Congress issued its instructions to Washington phrased in the most general terms. His first duty was quite clear—"to repair with all expedition to the colony of Massachusetts Bay and take charge of the army of the united colonists." Cambridge, the seat of the forces besieging Boston, lay some 350 miles away. By hard riding with his escort party the general could be expected to reach the Massachusetts encampment in perhaps six days.

Once in Cambridge, he was to make a count of all the men and stores that had been raised by the colonies. He was to determine as exactly as possible the strength of the British army in America. He was to hold all volunteers under arms, to feed them at the expense of the colonies, and to recruit further men as he saw fit, up to a number double that of the enemy. But the main instruction as to his military mission, these things done, was put by Congress in the following restrained language, which did not begin to suggest the length or bitterness of the war that lay ahead:

"You shall take every method in your power consistent with prudence, to destroy or make prisoners all persons who now are or who hereafter shall appear in arms against the good people of the united colonies."

The ink was scarcely dry on the Continental Congress's instructions to General Washington when fresh news from Boston hit Philadelphia like a bombshell. A bloody battle had taken place the previous Saturday, June 17th, between the entrenched New Englanders on Breed's Hill and Bunker Hill, and the attacking British regiments based in the town of Boston. Hundreds of dead from both sides were left on the battlefield, and more than one thousand were wounded. During the day the British had driven the colonials from their hastily fortified positions on Breed's Hill after the defenders' powder had run out. But the colonists had repulsed the regulars in two massive charges before yielding the strongpoint overlooking Boston harbor. Although the British troops succeeded in capturing a certain amount of ground, the colonial men under arms had gained a much more important victory, over fear of the British army's power. The battle had proved that the American colonists would stand up to the massed regulars, and they had fought like veterans.

It was imperative that Washington and his aides lose no time in reaching Cambridge. By June 23rd the New York Congress learned that the commander in chief was on his way from Philadelphia, and would pass through the city en route to Massachusetts. Major General Philip Schuyler was coming from Philadelphia with Washington to take command of the New York troops. To avoid lingering where a body of regulars might try to arrest him, Washington set a hard pace along the Delaware River, and thence across the level plain of New Jersey. On Saturday, June 24th, Philip Schuyler sent an express rider galloping ahead from New Brunswick with word for the New York Congress that he and General Washington would reach Newark, six miles from the New Jersey shore of the Hudson River, by Sunday morning. A delegation from New York should meet them, Schuyler wrote, and advise them as to the most prudent place at which to cross the river and approach New York City. On Schuyler's mind were both a display of respect for the commander in chief and the party's security. One could never tell whether a strong body of British troops had been landed in the neighborhood since the Bunker Hill battle. If they had, a Tory spy could ride fast to inform them of such a vulnerable prize.

The New York Congress sent a four-man delegation, accompanied by a few soldiers, to meet the generals at Newark, in order to conduct them across the Hudson from a landing on the New Jersey shore below the Palisades. Richard Montgomery was a logical choice for this duty. Yet hardly had the escort group taken to their boats when startling news was brought to the Exchange. The British Governor of New York, William Tryon, had arrived in port— today of all days. He was aboard the ship *Juliana* that had anchored in the shelter of Sandy Hook, a few miles down the coast from New York harbor. The governor planned to enter the city on Sunday, in the early afternoon. This was about the time when General Washington and his retinue would also be reaching New York.

What if the two parties should confront each other? Would there be an outbreak of firing between Governor Tryon's guard and the colonists who had taken to arms to fight the king's troops? For a while the deputies considered the possibility that a pitched battle might be fought right in the streets of New York—on a day when everyone would be outside in his finest clothes for church services and to welcome General Washington. What could be done to prevent the shedding of innocent blood?

At length it was decided that Colonel Lasher should head a strong body of militiamen, to stand in readiness with men posted at intervals along the waterfront. Whichever of the two dignitaries should arrive first, be it the newly appointed general of the Continental army, or the king's provincial governor, Colonel Lasher's forces should gather around the visitor "and wait on him as well as circumstances will allow." The strategy was designed to show respect to the governor, but to keep his party and that of General Washington well apart. It was a stroke of sheer ill fortune that brought this coincidence upon the city. But with dexterity and forbearance, if the hot-heads could be kept from shouting insults, New York could get through the day in safety.

The ministers in the New York pulpits on the morning of June 25th must have sensed the uneasiness and anticipation in the anxious congregations facing them, as the city impatiently awaited the arrival of general and governor. Outside the flags were flying, and drums were beating as militia companies assembled and marched through the streets. Everywhere people were out of the houses, gathering in groups to hear and discuss the latest news brought by runners from their vantage points near the waterfront. At length, shortly after noonday, the cry went up from those intently watching the New Jersey shore.

"Boats on the way! General Washington and his party are crossing the river!"

As the crowd, buzzing with excitement, swelled in numbers along the beach near the Hudson River docks, the boats came steadily closer, the long oars dipping and rising in unison as the rowers bent to their work. Closer and closer moved the little flotilla over the bright water, sparkling in the midsummer sun. The drums of the militia kept beating steadily, the church bells swung clanging in the belfries. Men shouted and waved their hats, ladies fluttered their handkerchiefs as parasols bobbed up and down in excited hands. As the boats pulled close, boys raced and tumbled over one another to help in heaving them ashore. Within a minute the gentlemen of the New York Congress were doffing their hats and bowing to General Washington.

Almost no one in New York had met the Virginian before. They saw an unusually tall, grave-faced man wearing a blue coat, with buff waistcoat and purple sash. Washington seemed to tower over most of his party, and though his face with its strong jaw and forehead reflected his full age, his vigor of motion gave the impression of a somewhat younger man. In contrast, Philip Schuyler, overweight and with thinning hair, his aspect that of a man constantly fatigued, locked several years Washington's senior, even though he was the younger of the two.

One hundred miles of riding in less than three days had been a wearying experience for the commander in chief and his party, so Washington was taken to the home of a member of the New York Congress, Leonard Lispenard, for refreshment and a rest. Lispenard's house was well chosen, for it lay a quarter mile beyond the edge of town, past the point where streets thick with houses gave way to open field and orchard. Lispenard's farm lay on a height above the Hudson shore, and was reached by the road that led northward to the village of Greenwich. On the island side of Lispenard's property a steep decline led down to a swampy area providing no access to the house or road. If, therefore, a raiding party of soldiers should make a sortie from Fort George in an attempt to apprehend General Washington, they would be forced to traverse a full mile or more of city streets first. Then they could approach Lispenard's only along the Greenwich road, a route that would be patrolled and protected as long as Washington would be in New York.

The road up the island provided an escape route, if one were needed.

While Washington was at this outlying point, Richard Montgomery joined his Janet at the house of her maternal grandfather, William Beekman, who lived in the city. Montgomery had been lodging there during the past month's meetings of the New York Congress, and Janet had come down the Hudson River to join him. Now, on this day of mixed rejoicing and uneasiness, Janet Livingston Montgomery must have felt within herself the conflicting emotions of the city and of this dubious time. For among her close friends the daughter of Judge Livingston counted both the daughter and the wife of Governor William Tryon. The three ladies had visited in one another's homes, and had often played cards and attended the theater together. There had been an increasing strain among them of late, quite naturally caused by the widening social gulf that followed the political passions of their men. But despite her personal friendships of years past, Janet Montgomery had no doubt of her own loyalties. She was a Livingston. She belonged in heart and tradition with the fight for freedom. And now she was the wife of a general in the colonial army.

Fortunately for the peace of New York that day, Governor Tryon did not arrive until late afternoon, when Washington was a good distance away. His boat landed at the Exchange, where the Tory gentlemen of the town gathered around, and Lasher's ceremonial guard saluted him as he stepped ashore. As discreetly as possible the governer's friends explained to him that although the military escort was, as he felt certain, meant to do him honor—the flags and bells and drums, and the crowds in the streets were saluting the presence of George Washington. Quietly and without seeking to attract attention, Tryon permitted his friends to lead him to the home of Hugh Wallace, a member of the governor's council. Through the evening and the following day, he found it wise to stay indoors and to watch the festivities outside through a curtained window.

Toward early evening, a grand parade of militia and cheering hundreds of people escorted General Washington from Lispenard's house through the streets to the city hall, the grand building at the head of Broad Way. Here he received the patriot leaders of New York, and in their presence, amid hearty applause, he handed military commissions to the two generals chosen by New York, Philip Schuyler and Richard Montgomery.

That evening, drawn apart from the noise of the celebrating crowd, this little group of men had a chance for a quiet discussion of their plans in the fight for liberty. In their conference over maps of the entire northeastern region of British America, the generals must have analyzed the military situation that confronted the united colonies, and determined at least tentatively on various courses of action. Building an army was clearly the first requisite. But there were other issues pending while the forces were being recruited, equipped and trained.

What should be the strategy if the British generals in Boston should receive heavy reinforcements, and with them should attack the army at Cambridge? Should New York itself be defended, even if a battle here meant ruin for the town? Or should a stand be made farther north on Manhattan Island, in open country? What if Governor Carleton should launch an attack from Canada? Should Lake Champlain be held at all costs, or would it be wise to retreat to Lake George?

The possibilities were discussed, and certain agreements reached. Yet every man present knew that they could be turned upside down within a few days by the uncontrollable fortunes of war, or by a host of events beyond their control. It was, at best, an uncertain kind of planning, in which almost every element was but dimly seen.

On one point Washington, Schuyler and Montgomery were fixed. The resolution adopted in Philadelphia that disclaimed any plan for an invasion of Canada would have to be discarded. When it was approved back on the first of June, its purpose was to forestall Ethan Allen and Benedict Arnold from launching a mad adventure that might turn the Canadians against the united colonies. But now the task was to prevent the troops under Carleton from invading New York. Should he possess the lakes and the upper Hudson Valley, he could then swing east and attack the New England colonies where they were lightly populated and lay exposed. From this position he might help the British generals now in Boston to crush all the colonial forces in the northeast. Schuyler and Montgomery would therefore take possession of the invasion route this summer, and go all the way to Montreal, if necessary, in order to do it.

The plan must have loomed up in Montgomery's mind as a repetition of his old campaigns under General Amherst and Monckton—the same route as in 1758 and 1759, the same wild, mountainous country to penetrate, the same strongpoints to be held or taken, the same strategic situation. Sixteen and seventeen years ago, however, he had been part of the best-drilled and most generously supplied fighting force in the world. This time he would be fighting against it. Now he would be among men and officers with almost no battle experience. And he himself, who had been no more

than an army captain only three years ago, found himself
a general. The realization of the responsibility thrust suddenly upon him must have chilled his blood.

At nine o'clock on Monday morning the deputies were
again in their places at the Exchange, as the Provincial
Congress went on with its preparations for the campaign.
An appeal from Albany for seventy-eight blankets for
Albany County men holding the fort at Lake George, where
even the midsummer nights were cold. Final approval of all
details in the contract with Watkeys and Boyd to make
muskets, and payment of fifty pounds to enable them to
start. Dealing with Forbes and Hoagland, saddlers, to manufacture cartridge-boxes, slings and belts for the New York
troops. Reading letters on the state of affairs in Massachusetts and other colonies. Raising money to pay the
troops in the north, in order to keep them from deserting.
Preparing a message to the Indians lurking in the forests
above Albany. Choosing a camping ground on the edge of
town for Connecticut troops under Brigadier General
Wooster, who were arriving shortly to report for duty under
Schuyler.

At half past two in the afternoon, General Washington
entered the hall in response to an invitation from the congress. Only yesterday he was the center of a rejoicing, cheering throng of patriots who saw in him the figure of leader
and protector. Yet today he listened to a brief, formal address from the Provincial Congress, reminding the commander in chief that its grant of authority to him was closely
limited, in purpose and time.

"We rejoice in the appointment of a gentleman from
whose abilities and virtues we are taught to expect both
security and peace," the address declared, in praise of Wash-

ington. "Confiding in you, Sir, and in the worthy Generals immediately under your command, we have the most flattering hopes of success in the glorious struggle for American liberty!" However, it continued, whenever the struggle for an accommodation with England shall be decided, the New York Congress said it felt "the fullest assurance . . . that you will cheerfully resign the important deposit committed into your hands, and resume the character of our worthiest citizen."

Washington had been aware for some time that many colonists feared the power of any standing army, foreign or domestic. History had all too often proved that a general who conquers in the field could be led by ambition to try to dominate the people from whom he had drawn his strength. When Washington rose to reply to the address, he therefore made clear the limit to his ambition. In common with the New York deputies, he said, he deplored "the unhappy necessity" of taking up arms. The general assured them he would seek "the re-establishment of peace and harmony" with England equally with "the fatal but necessary operations of war." As to his own future, the general pledged in these words that he and his officers were civilians at heart, with no ambition to rule:

"When we assumed the soldier, we did not lay aside the citizen. And we shall most sincerely rejoice with you in that happy hour when the establishment of American liberty, on the most firm and solid foundations, shall enable us to return to our private stations in the bosom of a free, peaceful, and happy country."

By five o'clock, with the sun standing high in the west, General Washington and his party, escorted by several companies of New York militia, were again in the saddle, riding

northward from the city up Manhattan Island. It was close
to sunset when they crossed the height of land near the Blue
Bell. Doubtless the long, rocky ridge to the left, which
Montgomery had considered a logical point to fortify when
the time was ripe, must have caught Washington's eye.
From this vantage point he could appreciate the difficulty
of holding all this terrain against a determined attack—
unless the colonies could raise a mighty armed force to
meet it.

As he rode onward, down the decline that led to the
bridge over Harlem Kill, Washington could reflect, too, on
the fact that this was territory where artillery would play
the role of king, to the infantry's traditional role of "queen
of battles," as the saying went. This was no wooded country suitable for Indian-style fighting, as on that fateful day
twenty years ago near Fort Duquesne, when General Brad-
dock had met defeat. Here the force with the guns on the
heights would dominate, but only if they had the regiments
to protect them.

Nightfall found the party at King's Bridge, and here they
took their rest. The following morning Washington was hard
on the Boston Post Road, heading for Cambridge and the
siege of Boston.

4

On to Canada!

ON Tuesday, June 27th, Washington and his party were already riding through Connecticut on the road to Cambridge when the Continental Congress formally resolved to launch the campaign which Generals Washington, Schuyler and Montgomery had discussed two days before.

Canada was to be invaded by armed force. But the invasion would be carried out purely for defensive reasons. The Congress wanted it clearly understood that the enemy was the British army—not the people of Canada. Neither the Indians nor the white settlers, be they new arrivals from England or the French-speaking habitants, as the English called the older colonists, were to be considered hostile to the united colonies. In fact, Congress hoped to win them to the cause of liberty, and to welcome their delegates in Philadelphia as representatives of a fourteenth member of the colonial union.

The object of the campaign was to prevent the British forces now in Canada from attacking the other provinces. The strategy of going on the offensive for self-defense was due to the nature of this country. Through mile upon mile of wooded wilderness, containing only a few isolated settlements, the lakes and rivers provided the only real highroads. Freedom to move at will would lie with the force that would dominate the lakes.

Congress directed Schuyler to move as swiftly as possible to the Lake Champlain forts, to size up the strength both of the colonial forces and of the enemy, and determine, if he could, "the disposition of the Canadians, and the Indians of Canada." He was to build a fleet of gunboats that would enable the Americans to control Lake Champlain. The Continental Congress resolved that because Governor Carleton, the British commander in Quebec, was preparing to invade the colonies and was "instigating the Indian Nations to take up the hatchet against them, Major General Schuyler do exert his utmost power to destroy or take all vessels, boats or floating batteries, preparing by said Governor or by his order.

The resolution of Congress went on to state that if Schuyler found it practicable, and at the same time "not disagreeable to the Canadians," he was to "take possession of St. John's, Montreal, and any other parts of the country, and pursue any other measures in Canada, which may have a tendency to promote the peace and security of these Colonies." This was a sweeping mandate, authorizing Schuyler to lead his army just as far as he could. Indeed, the course advocated a few weeks earlier by Benedict Arnold and Ethan Allen, and rejected—to "rise on eagle's wings" and to "take Canada"—now had the official blessing of the Congress in Philadelphia.

In New York City the pace of preparation was quickened both by the grim battle news from Boston and by the in-

spiration of General Washington's visit. Now there was no
hesitation. The decision to wage organized war against
tyranny had been taken. Save for a handful of scorning
Tories, most of New York hurried about the business of
preparing to fight. Schuyler was nominally in command, but
Richard Montgomery found himself making most of the
day-to-day decisions of organizing both the expedition into
Canada and the defense of New York City.

Washington had given the New York generals a free hand
in choosing their own subordinate commanders for regiments, battalions and companies. At first, a good many
propertied gentlemen hesitated to take leadership in the
colonial army. Some of them had served well in the past in
the war against the French and in the peacetime militia.
Then they had British organization, British supply-lines and
the security of being on the side of established authority.

But taking part in an army of rebellion made many of
them feel uneasy. It would be an uphill struggle merely to
organize and equip each military unit, and there was no
time to waste in persuading the reluctant. The first volunteers for commissioned rank who appeared to have the necessary spirit and intelligence were named as colonels, majors
and captains.

Montgomery could not be bothered with petty complaints
from some that their military rank was beneath their social
status, as they conceived it. He was not happy about accepting certain officers who appeared to be just prestige-seekers,
who thought more of their rank and wearing a fine uniform
than of fighting to win. But the general had to take the best
candidates available, and hope that he could make something of them. So the roster of officers for the New York
regiments was a mixed lot, that included eager tradesmen

and small merchants, as well as gentlemen of fine manners and large land-holdings.

For this new-style army, to be made up of volunteer soldiers, Montgomery realized that he needed officers who would actively lead and inspire men. Only yesterday, Britain herself had furnished an outstanding example of such an officer. In common with every Englishman who had fought in America, Richard Montgomery revered the memory of the late General James Wolfe, the conqueror of Quebec. In fact, New York had erected a Wolfe Memorial on the northwest edge of the city. The hero of the Plains of Abraham was born into a family without great property or title. Wolfe's success was shining proof that high birth is not a necessity in the making of a great battle leader. Spirit, intelligence, perseverance and, if need be, personal courage of the highest order count for much more. If the British soldier, who was usually impressed into the service by force, would respond to the leadership of a man like Wolfe, it was all the more necessary for New York to have officers who would inspire and lead, rather than whip their troops from behind. For the colony had almost none of the powers of forcible persuasion over volunteer soldiers that the British crown held over its soldiers and sailors.

Two days after Washington's departure, Montgomery found a few moments in which to write a brief letter to Judge Livingston. In it he touched on a number of concerns that filled his waking hours. He had been assigned by the assembly to find an artisan with the skill to make a brass fieldpiece. Yet where he could locate a cannon-maker in or near the town no one knew. Long hours had to be spent with a clerk preparing lists of supplies to be bought—if any shop had them for sale. Subordinate officers had to be taught their duties quickly enough that they could in turn recruit and drill the rank-and-file volunteers. Military surgeons had to be secured among the doctors of the province, and they had to be supplied with chests of surgical instruments and medicines.

Where in all New York was there an experienced artillery officer? And an engineer capable of building a fort? It was a succession of hurried, wearying days, filled with frustration, as Montgomery found the practical business of building up General Schuyler's army loaded heavily onto his shoulders.

He would try soon to manage a hurried trip home, Montgomery wrote to his father-in-law, to bring Janet and one of her younger sisters out of the city: "I cannot remain long there as the Continental Congress have done me the melancholy honor of appointing me a brigadier. I am most truly at the public service, but could have wished to have served in a private capacity."

He would appoint two of Janet's younger brothers, Henry and John Livingston, as junior officers, he wrote their father, and would try to put them in separate regiments. As for the news from Boston, following up the first accounts of the fighting at Breed's Hill and Bunker Hill, Montgomery was skeptical. "The truth," he remarked, "cannot be expected from either side." He concluded from what he knew that the British regulars could not have won a great advantage in the fight, "or they would have pushed further."

Montgomery thought that the regulars might attack New York City soon. Since the governor's arrival, several British transports lay off Sandy Hook without trying to land their troops. Under cover of darkness, a few port victualers tried to row out to the ships with supplies for sale, and just as regularly were forced to run an angry gauntlet of patriots patrolling in small boats. On June 30th the skirmishing in the harbor ended when the transports hauled anchor and sailed off in the direction of Boston, leaving New York to breathe a little more easily.

Governor Tryon, however, stayed aboard a man-of-war in New York harbor, where he would remain a danger to the patriots. Montgomery wrote to Robert Livingston that, "I believe Mr. Tryon means to conduct himself with prudence. He will, however, be well watched. . . . It is possible I shan't remain much longer in this town. *You know why.* Schuyler talks of setting out on Monday."

By July 3rd a force of 1,500 Connecticut men under General Wooster had camped at Elliot's farm on the edge of town, and were ready to move north as soon as Schuyler and Montgomery would provide equipment and boats. On that day Wooster joined the two New York generals in a review of Colonel Lasher's battalion of city militia. The *New York Gazette & Weekly Mercury* informed its readers that the review was held "in the presence of a very respectable number of the principal ladies and gentlemen of the town. They [the militia] went through the exercise and evolutions with the greatest order, alertness and decorum." To Montgomery, this was purely parade-ground show, of value in strengthening civilian morale, perhaps, but no sign at all that the paraders were an expeditionary force that would fight.

It was important, as he knew, to cement the best possible relations with the sister colony, because New York and Connecticut had in the past disputed some of the frontier territories in the north. As a gesture of gratitude and goodwill to the Connecticut forces who had come to the aid of

New York, the officers of the city invited General Wooster and his officers to a gala dinner and entertainment. The affair was held on July 5th in the field adjoining the house of Samuel Francis. According to the *Gazette & Mercury,* "the day was spent in utmost harmony, and many toasts were drunk." Probably the same could be said of most of the celebrants. Readers could visualize the talk and cheering becoming steadily more boisterous under the prompting of full tankards, with each officer seeking to outdo the others in wit and defiance as he offered a toast. The place rang with such cries as:

"The King—better counsellors to him!"

"General Washington, and the army under his command!"

"Conquest and laurels to all those heroes who draw their swords in support of freedom!"

"May the enemies of America be turned into saltpetre, and go off in hot blasts!"

"The daughters of America in the arms of their brave defenders ONLY!"

Finally, the most wordy toast of all, in tribute to the farmers of Lexington and Concord:

"The glorious Nineteenth of April, when the brave Americans convinced General Gage and the friends of tyranny that they dare fight and conquer also!"

Doubtless the memory of that July day of hot defiance of Britain's armed power stayed with the participants for weeks later as they drilled and outfitted the troops, and as one company after another sailed from New York up the Hudson River to Albany, then marched northward to camp near Saratoga. Philip Schuyler moved forward with the early contingents. Montgomery followed with the main body of New York troops as soon as they had the minimal equipment for taking the field. Others were still being organized and equipped as he sailed, and were scheduled to embark as soon as the boats were available.

Almost everything required to put an army of three thousand men into the Lake Champlain country was in short supply. But at least the Continental Congress had managed in early July to send fifty quarter-kegs of gunpowder to New York, to be forwarded immediately to Ticonderoga. And this encouraging shipment reached the fort about the time Schuyler appeared there to survey the scene and to gather intelligence of the enemy strength and whereabouts.

"No maneuver appears to me more necessary than an immediate movement to St. John's," Schuyler wrote to the Continental Congress from Ticonderoga on July 27th. "But how to get there?"

The general reported that a lake sloop and the schooner *Liberty* were in American hands on the lake. Further, he said that a party of Indians and French Canadians near the Ile la Motte, at the north end of the lake, had informed the sloop captain "that Governor Carleton had in vain attempted to prevail upon the savages to act against us; that the Canadians would be neuter, perhaps act in our favor." He went on to describe the fortification of St. John's by a ditch and stout pickets, behind which a garrison of some four hundred and fifty soldiers were mounting cannon.

Taken as a whole, Schuyler's message was the first of a long series he was to send from the theater of military operations that conveyed his gloomy, negative outlook that amounted almost to hopelessness. Schuyler was a cautious man, who was trying to weigh his chances with care so as not to run needless risks. If he had the quality of boldness and daring, he kept it well hidden. In this dispatch to Congress, as in many that were to follow, the strength of the enemy was formidable, where as Schuyler's own command was riddled with weaknesses and shortcomings. It was in Schuyler's nature to paint the enemy larger than life and the enemy's chances for success in the most optimistic colors. The Continentals, on the other hand, received the dark strokes of Schuyler's descriptive brush. [And running like a thread through one dispatch after another was Schuyler's indecision, his endless capacity for throwing his problems back on the Provincial Congress, or on the Continental Congress—neither of which was in a position to make an on-the-spot decision.\

"But how to get there?"—Schuyler complained, immediately after stating that he thought he should move at once to St. John's. His letter spelled out a list of his difficulties, with no suggestion of how Congress could solve them:

> "All the craft I am possessed of will not carry at the most more than five hundred and fifty men. Nor are any of the stores mentioned in a former letter of mine, as yet arrived here. It is probable that they have not yet left New York, and without them I cannot proceed, even if I had the boats. For my whole stock of powder will be less than three tons when that from Philadelphia arrives. I must necessarily not fire a gun without certain execution. . . ."

Schuyler's catalogue of miseries went on to include his lack of entrenching tools and food stores. He pledged to "move the moment I am in a condition for it." Then he predicted that this would probably lead to defeat. For even should he capture St. John's, Schuyler speculated, he would probably use up all his powder in the assault. He would therefore be forced to retreat not only from that fort, but also from Fort Ticonderoga, leaving the British in command of the entire lake. Thus, Schuyler worried himself into a losing campaign, even before one shot had been fired. A gloomy prospect indeed, from the commanding general of a force with the mission to attack!

Richard Montgomery, who had reached Albany late in July, was in a quite different mood from his commanding general. While Schuyler dwelt on every possibility that could go wrong, Montgomery instead seized on everything that could be turned to advantage. As a veteran soldier who was a stranger neither to fear nor to victory, Montgomery never forgot the basic rule in judging an enemy: that he is made of common clay, like all men. To overrate him is the error of the fearful.

The foe, though he may be out of sight and hearing at the moment, is usually just as weary, as deprived of necessities, and as frightened, as one's own troops. If our men have been feeding badly on half-spoiled pork and last year's wormy flour—so have the British regulars. They, too, must measure their powder with care. Their ranks, as well as ours, have their share of cowards. A march of twenty miles is as exhausting to the redcoat as to the colonist, and perhaps more so. Looking straight into the cannon's muzzle is as terrifying to him as it is to our men.

In contrast to Schuyler's tendency to magnify his difficulties so as to be almost immobilized by his fearful hesitations, Montgomery was constantly on the alert for what he could accomplish with the means at hand. He could see setbacks ahead, but to him a defeat need not lead to a disaster. He was willing to make decisions, to take action in the face of difficulties even if conditions were not perfect.

"Should the Canadians relish the intended visit," he

wrote to Robert early in August, "it will effectively secure us from Indian hostilities. Should we have success it will show our strength to the world." The Continental army would be greatly extended in that case, and a large force would be required to hold any gains in Canada the following season. But even if Carleton should counterattack, the New York and Connecticut forces would probably be strong enough by that time to hold the southern end of Lake Champlain against any force that Carleton could command.

In his letters to his brother-in-law, Montgomery was indirectly helping the civilians of the Continental Congress understand the true state of military affairs, at least as he saw them, in the confusing months of half-war and half-peace of 1775. And in a certain measure he must have counteracted the pessimism of Schuyler, though without showing disrespect for his superior.

Montgomery's letters sparkled with precise, practical proposals and suggestions on how to bring the ill-prepared colonies to arms in a hurry. After his journey up the Hudson River to Albany, for example, Montgomery advised Robert that "I observed with pleasure the river may be made impassable" at the narrow S-shaped stretch in the Highlands, near Bear Mountain. This could be done by means of a floating boom of heavy logs and an iron chain. The boom should be covered by strong artillery positions on the heights. It could be attached on one bank only, and allowed to lie along the shore without interrupting navigation. Then, should hostile ships attempt to sail upstream, it could be easily closed on the flood tide. The ships would then be caught in a trap, and the batteries could rain down fire upon them.

Montgomery cautioned Robert that Congress had made

an error in recommending that forts along the Hudson be built of stone. The united colonies had neither time nor manpower for fortress-building in the European style. Log forts, Montgomery wrote, could be made much faster and cheaper, and each could be made very strong with a garrison of only one hundred men.

As for overcoming the shortage of powder and shot, the most pressing lack throughout the colonies, Montgomery made a novel suggestion: the crossbow. Had anyone in Philadelphia thought of reviving this ancient weapon, that required no gunpowder nor iron? A good bowman could shoot a half-dozen bolts in the time a soldier needed to swab out his musket and ram home a new load of powder and shot. And the crossbow could be as deadly accurate as any firearm.

Montgomery's busy mind and pen turned to Governor Tryon, who was still aboard his ship in New York harbor, nursing a menacing anger against the New York townspeople. "I am afraid he is carrying on some secret designs," the young general wrote to his brother-in-law. "Would it not be doing Mr. Tryon a service to conduct him to Hartford?" There, separated by a hundred miles from the strategic Hudson route he would be "out of the way of mischief."

Finally, on the quality of his troops, Montgomery showed himself uncertain, but hopeful of improvement: "I can't tell whether we can expect the troops to fight. I desire nothing more. I think the want of dexterity in handling arms may be amply supplied by resolution and vigor."

During most of August the army was being equipped, trained and moved northward toward Canada, unit by unit, like an extended swarm of men climbing in clusters toward the top of a giant, rocky cliff. Schuyler was at the apex,

Fort Ticonderoga, where he viewed the scene with dismal eye. For weeks he relayed to Congress a stream of pessimistic reports, which he had picked up from individual travelers in the lake country, testifying to the strength of the enemy at and near St. John's. According to Schuyler's messages, British gunboats under construction there were largely completed, and measured close to sixty feet in length; there were between fifty and sixty carpenters working at St. John's; the boats would mount sixteen to eighteen guns each; between thirty and forty heavy fort guns, including 18- and 24-pounders, were on the way to St. John's from nearby Chambly; St. John's itself was fortified by a deep ditch, heavy earthworks and a double row of log pickets "as big as a man's thigh"—and so forth.

Meanwhile, Schuyler complained, he had to set the tiny handful of carpenters at his disposal to building boats, to the neglect of repairing the fort. He described Ticonderoga as "in the most defenseless condition. Perhaps," the irresolute general added in his message to Congress, "it might be proper to send a small committee to examine the country, and report whether this or any other place ought to be fortified, in case it should become necessary."

In effect, the general was casting doubt on the wisdom of his entire mission.

Philip Schuyler was an ill man, whose outlook and judgment were affected by his physical suffering. Probably neither the New York nor the Philadelphia Congresses knew that Schuyler, though only forty-two, was already heir to ailments more common among older men—hereditary gout, rheumatism and bilious fevers. Doubtless the rigors of the journey to Ticonderoga and the absence of comforts to which he was accustomed in his palatial home had irritated the conditions already present in his tired body. It is possible that Richard Montgomery had caught wind of Schuyler's true state of mind and health long weeks before, and was referring indirectly to it when he had asked Robert: "But has he *strong nerves?*"

From New York by boat to Albany, then to Saratoga where the Hudson diminishes to a stream, and thence by narrow roads and rough wagon trails through the forest to Lake George, Montgomery for weeks kept hurrying the troops along. The summer was already growing very late as he finally left subordinates in charge of the supply line, and moved rapidly up the chain of posts himself in order to join Schuyler at Fort Ticonderoga. By August 10th, having passed through the last of the settled parts of the province, he felt impelled to send an order back to the commander at Albany regarding the conduct of the troops. Looting and careless destruction by the passing soldiers, as he well knew from years of campaigning, must be halted at the outset. Otherwise, an army would sacrifice the support of the populace behind it and make enemies of those who would otherwise be friends.

"I entreat you," Montgomery wrote, "that individuals may not suffer in their property. Let no pains be omitted to impress the men with just notions of our duty to society and how infamous it is in us, who have arms in our hands for the protection of our fellow citizens, to betray that trust by any violation of their rights."

By mid-August Montgomery reached Fort Ticonderoga. What a contrast it offered now to the wartime fort he had known sixteen years before! During the war with the French it was a new fort, its ditches steeply graded, its sharpened log pickets in place, its gun embrasures bristling with cannon.

So powerful had this fort been when the French held it that they had beaten off a massive British attack in the summer of 1758, with great loss of life for the attackers. Only because the French were outmaneuvered and outflanked in the following year had they withdrawn from Fort Carillon, as they called it, and the British virtually walked in to possess it. The new name, Ticonderoga, which they gave this strongpoint, came from the Indian term meaning "Tail-of-the-Lake," since it stood where the long, tapering southern end of Champlain almost touched the upper end of Lake George.

Montgomery sized the situation up as both encouraging and alarming. The fort was pretty much of a shambles. Sixteen years' snow and rain had largely leveled out the protective ditches and rotted away part of the picket walls. The log buildings were much decayed. Indeed, this fort had been treated as a minor outpost rather than a strongpoint during the years of peace. But the major part of the army was now here or would soon arrive. The New York and Connecticut troops were moving forward rapidly, at three-day intervals. It looked, at last, as if the Lake Champlain expeditionary force would soon be ready for action.

The men were now armed, and uniformed after a fashion. Those who reached Ticonderoga were dressed in the primary uniform garment, a long-tailed coat faced with trim colors that showed on lapels and cuffs. Most of the rest of the soldier's costume he had worn on enlisting—the low-brim three-cornered hat that would fend off much of the sun and rain, shirt of rough cotton or wool, cotton drill or buckskin waistcoat and breeches, leggings, homespun wool socks, and plain brown or black shoes. Each regiment was distinguished by the color of its coat and facing. These varied from blue coat with red facing for the First New York Regiment, under Colonel Alexander McDougall, through various combinations of light and dark brown, gray, and other coats of shades definitely less conspicuous than the bright red worn by the British regulars.

Most of the soldiers carried their own muskets and powder horns, and each had been supplied with enough powder and shot to enable him to fire at least a dozen rounds. Every man had been outfitted with a canvas haversack, blanket, wooden canteen and cartridge box. Other personal articles such as eating knife, spoon, change of socks and sometimes a Bible made up the rest of his kit.

Because most of the men's weapons were hunting pieces rather than military muskets, only a few were equipped with bayonet sockets and bayonets. The British army had proved, in victory upon victory, that after a line of troops had fired a volley, a bayonet charge could have a devastating effect on the enemy. As a result, the regulars were equipped as a matter of course with these frightful impaling weapons. Until the Americans could be likewise armed, the colonial officers were pressed to teach their men to parry the bayonet thrust with their own musket barrel, then close with the enemy in hand-to-hand struggle. But the volunteers' cold fear of the British bayonet was hard to overcome.

As the hasty boat-building and improvised training went on, the daylight hours of August were becoming noticeably shorter than those of midsummer. Nights in the Champlain country brought a penetrating chill to the men who slept on the ground without tents. By day, however, Ticonderoga was a beautiful place, which tempted visitor and soldier to linger as long as possible while the weather held. The blue waters of Lake Champlain and Lake George, which almost touched here, sparkled in the August sun as they stretched away between the varying light greens of leafy hardwoods and the darker hemlock and pine that crowded down to the water's edge. Here and there the sun caught the bright, thin scar of white birch trunks, that appeared as tiny scratches against the green hills. Farther back, the distant mountains faded into dark blue and gray, in contrast to the white, cumulus castles of cloud that floated almost daily over the lake country. This was an outdoorsman's paradise, the domain of wild deer, rabbit, game birds and lake fish, which provided the best fare the soldiers had enjoyed since leaving home.

Tempting as it was to remain, there was no time to waste in moving up Lake Champlain. Although Montgomery had been distressed to find that both forts, at Ticonderoga and at Crown Point, were indeed in the sorry state that Schuyler had described, the boat-building had been moving forward. It looked as if by the last week in August there would be sufficient craft ready to carry two regiments at a time to the north end of Lake Champlain. Although two of the four New York regiments had not yet arrived, Montgomery and Schuyler had close to half their prospective army at the lake now, as well as five hundred of the New Hampshire men who called themselves the Green Mountain Boys.*

Only a few days after Montgomery had reached Ticonderoga, General Schuyler turned over the command to him and returned to Saratoga to attend his wife, who was seriously ill. The general himself seemed in very poor health and great bodily pain. While his superior was away, Montgomery determined to move the expedition forward as far

* Vermont, or "Green Mountain" in French, was still part of New Hampshire colony in 1775.

as the Ile aux Noix. This island, with its earthen breast-works prepared long ago by the French, was placed like a stopper that almost closed the great bottle of Lake Champlain at its narrow, tapering northern end. In fact, at this point the lake and the Sorel River merged into each other. Here, if his gunners would do their business, he could seal off the lake from any British boats, which would have to pass by on the way up the Sorel from St. John's.

"Every intelligence from Canada evinces the necessity of a vigorous and speedy effort to crush their naval armament before it gets abroad, however ill prepared we may be to encounter a well appointed enemy," Montgomery wrote in one of his frequent dispatches. His decision to move, even without Schuyler, was in keeping with his activist character. It was Montgomery's way to take action that he considered necessary, then report to Congress that he had done so, and why. In contrast, the slow-moving Schuyler seemed to throw almost every decision back at Congress, without deciding or acting on his own. As late as August 19th, while in Saratoga, Schuyler was again writing to the New York Congress asking that he be told whether or not Fort Ticonderoga should be prepared for defense:

"If it be determined that Ticonderoga is the place to be kept, I should know it the soonest possible, that such men as may be left there may be set to work in making the necessary repairs."

By August 28th, Schuyler still being absent, Montgomery set out from Ticonderoga with the first New York regiment, the fifth Connecticut regiment, and a company of artillery commanded by Captain Samuel Mott. Two days of stormy north winds delayed the expedition at Crown Point, but on the thirty-first the wind turned and the boats were able to proceed, by sail and oars, toward the Ile la Motte. During the three days' journey up the lake the wooded hills on either side gave way to flat ground, much of it marshy, marked by thin stands of alder and willow. If one knew the Indian trails around the worst of the bogs, it was country in which a traveler could move with relative speed, though he would have mud-caked feet and legs to show for it.

Schuyler caught up with Montgomery's corps at the island early on September 4th, having trailed him by an interval of a day's journey all the way from Ticonderoga. Montgomery, seeing Schuyler after a three-week interval, was shocked at the piteously ill condition he presented. He recognized that the older man must have been forcing himself at a pace he could not long continue. Perhaps it was pride in the commander that demanded he be present when his command was moving in close to the enemy. But it was clear to Montgomery that Schuyler should not have been in the field at all.

Whatever his feelings and physical suffering, Schuyler ordered the regiments to take to the boats at once, and by late evening, aided by the gathering current of the mouth of the Sorel River, they reached the Ile aux Noix. Here the old fort, first built by the French, lay completely abandoned. From its earthworks, however, the Americans would command a field of fire over the scant 250 yards of water on both sides, where the placid lake narrowed to become the slow-moving upper reaches of the Sorel. The boats had brought up only four 12-pound artillery pieces, which fired a cannonball scarcely bigger than a large man's fist. This was not artillery to sink a heavy vessel at a distance, where only one shot in ten might score a hit. But at the close range possible here, if the British should try to push past the island fort against the current, the troops could do great damage even with musket-fire and the small field pieces, because every shot would strike home.

Meanwhile, heavier artillery was on the way from Ticonderoga. The American force spent a full day preparing their position for defense. So far, they had won the race for the Champlain bottleneck. But could they hold it? Generals Schuyler and Montgomery and the regimental commanders determined they must push forward to St. John's to take possession of the heavily armed vessels being built there, or to destroy them in place. Only then would the major part of their mission to protect the lake country be safely accomplished.

With two of the four 12-pounders placed in a ready-fire position in the forward boats, the flotilla set out on the morning of September 6th and quietly drifted, with help from the oars, downstream toward the St. John's fort. For many weeks the Americans had been hearing reports of its formidable strength—its fortifications, the firepower of its cannon, and the number of trained men entrenched there for its defense. They knew that the British, on their side, were completely informed of the invasion force, since throughout these northern woodlands, from Saratoga all the way to this point, lurked Indians and trappers who traveled almost unseen and carried news of what they observed with them. If Canadians sympathetic to the colonists' cause had been steadily supplying the Americans with intelligence on the activity of the regulars, other Canadians were doing likewise in the opposite direction.

About two miles upstream from St. John's, the American boats glided around a curve and came suddenly into full view of the fort. For the inexperienced volunteers in the boats it was a moment for cold fear. They had been seen. Would they now be bombarded?

The answer was not long in coming from the fort. The apprehensive soldiers in the flotilla saw several flashes of fire, followed by quick puffs of smoke belching from the distant cannon. Then the dull, booming explosions, like threatening summer thunder, struck their ears. Within a few seconds fear gave way to good spirits and mocking shouts of derision, as one shot after another splashed harmlessly into the stream, wide of the mark, or crashed among the trees on shore. The salvo was merely a greeting, which was not repeated. A short distance below, the boats put in to shore and the entire American force debarked under cover of the woods.

General Schuyler was suffering such pain by this time that he remained in his boat with a detail of guards, while Montgomery took command of the units that were to advance on the fort. The lead company had gone about a quarter mile forward when firing and war whoops rang out through the woods. The Americans suddenly found they had been caught in an ambush by a mixed party of Indians and British regulars. Lead balls from hidden men's muskets whizzed menacingly close to the colonials as most of the men took cover as best they could behind trees and in low points on the ground. To Montgomery's disgust, some of the men took to their heels in craven fear, and were not halted until they had run into the rear companies moving forward in support. But for the most part the recruits and their equally inexperienced officers held fast, and traded fire with the enemy.

It shortly became apparent that there was no great force opposing them, but merely an advance party with a mission to delay their approach and to warn the fort that the invaders were close by. After the first shot from each musket had been fired, the Indians, redcoats and Americans alike were largely occupied with swabbing, loading fresh powder and shot, cleaning the fire-hole, priming the pan with powder, and only then searching out a fresh target through the trees. Desultory fire kept up for about fifteen minutes. Then the ambush group withdrew by degrees toward St. John's, leaving seven Indians dead and several wounded. The American casualties were in about the same proportion.

It was the first engagement of the campaign, though hardly more than a skirmish. But as the wounded displayed their bandages that evening among their comrades, the men realized today they had become the equals of their fellow countrymen in Boston, who had traded shots with the regulars in true military fashion. Now, baptized by hot fire, they were no longer raw recruits in training, but soldiers.

Montgomery's corps pulled back at nightfall, far enough to be out of range of the fort's cannon. The general had already found out through his spyglass what he had come forward to learn—that the first of the enemy ships, which mounted sixteen guns, was almost ready to sail. Since he could not seize the vessel quickly by a land approach, or destroy it with his feeble pair of 12-pounders, the wise course would be to return the short twelve miles to the Ile aux Noix and prepare to stop the ship there with a log boom. Then he could return to St. John's, undertake a serious siege and destroy this vital outpost of British army power in Canada. For he had heard from numerous reports that the majority of Britain's soldiers in the entire province of Quebec were stationed here at St. John's and at Fort Chambly, which lay another ten miles downstream. If these two posts could be isolated and taken, the rest of Canada would lie open to the American army.

Writing the next day to his Janet from the Ile aux Noix, Richard Montgomery confided to her that he was more concerned now over the men's discipline and soldierly morale than he was about his lack of powder and arms. Describing the fighting the day before, he wrote:

> "We had a little skirmish with the Indians—two very good officers wounded and nine or ten privates killed. A good deal of confusion in the action. The Yorkers are little acquainted with wood-fighting; the Connecticut men behaved well for the most part, but in the evening when some shells were thrown from the fort, they showed a degree of *apprehension* that displeased me much. But I hope and believe it will wear off with a little practice.
>
> "The general thought proper to remove a little farther off with the boats and vessels, and they embarked with such confusion that can only be palliated by saying they are young troops. I have endeavored to make them ashamed of themselves, and hope this won't happen again. I believe I am on a tolerable footing with them.
>
> "Poor Schuyler is in so miserable a state of health as to make him an object of compassion."

Montgomery could not be certain of it as he wrote, but his concern over the men's behavior was well founded. Their inexperience, their ignorance of military behavior and the downright cowardice of many in the ranks were to cause him infinite grief as long as he held this command. Furthermore, the entire burden was to rest on his shoulders. For General Philip Schuyler on that one day had heard the last shot he was to hear for the entire campaign.

❧ 5 ❧

"Let Us Have Rum, My Dear General"

RICHARD MONTGOMERY knew that every hour the colonial army spent at the Ile aux Noix was time which the enemy turned to his advantage. Day by day the defenses of Fort St. John's were being strengthened; every day the armed ships were nearer to sailing. If the Americans should delay too long, they might never be able to capture the fort and vessels before winter would close down upon them.

Three days after he had withdrawn from St. John's, Montgomery embarked again on the Sorel River, this time with a force of eight hundred men. While the remainder of the army was completing the log boom at the Ile aux Noix, Montgomery's party was to surround the fort and cut off its communication with the outside. This would mean putting one force ashore on the east bank of the Sorel to prevent the British from slipping across the river. The main body would then deploy in a great half-circle around the fort from the south and west, all the way to the river bank a mile or two north of the fort. Once the ring would be closed, the fort would be denied any reinforcements and supplies that had been reaching it from Fort Chambly, ten miles downstream, and from the town of Montreal, eighteen miles away to the northwest.

[General Schuyler was now so ill that he could scarcely leave his cot, and in effect he had handed over command of the army in the field to Montgomery.] Within another week Schuyler set out by boat for Fort Ticonderoga, where he hoped that more comfortable quarters and better food might bring him back to health. Now Montgomery was on his own.

Landing at dusk on September 10th, well upstream from the fort, Montgomery ordered a mixed force of New England and New York men under Colonel Ritzema to move out through the dark to the northwest and encircle Fort St. John's. This was boggy country. As the men plodded cautiously forward through the gloom, they came upon places where they sank to their knees in the heavy clay soil. They bumped into trees, or into the man ahead. They scraped their faces on bushes into which they stumbled. To all of the volunteers this was an unknown, mysterious and terrifying place, even more so at night than by daylight. The ambush of a few days before made them wary. In their imagination, the black shadows concealed lurking Indians armed with scalping hatchets, and waiting regulars with their cruel bayonets fixed for the charge. The advancing Americans, still untried in battle, were certain that the defenders of St. John's, silent and unseen, were watching their approach with a thousand eyes. At any moment a fusillade might shatter the night and cut them down like so much ripe wheat.

Despite the men's fear of the enemy hidden all about them, the forward elements of the column finally reached

the outer breastworks of the fort on the north side, close to
the Chambly road. Scarcely were they in position, at about
ten o'clock, when scattered musket-fire broke out a few hundred yards back along the route of approach. Ritzema and
a small party moved back to investigate, whereupon the
entire center of the American line fled in panic. The green
troops apparently believed that their approaching comrades
were a force of British regulars. Within a minute virtually
the entire line of encirclement had collapsed. Almost every
man who heard another crashing through the underbrush
fled as if the devil himself in a red coat were after him.
Some scattered widely through the marshes, splashing
through water up to their chests, and only stopped running
when they had reached the original assembly point. There
they faced a determined line of riflemen, who were drawn
up under command of the officers to halt the panic by a
show of force.

Dismayed and disgusted, Montgomery rallied the men
and officers, and sent them back to encircle Fort St. John's
once again. Within an hour another panic ensued, that
brought the young general to the point of despair. These
troops were afraid of their own shadows, and of the noise
made by their own comrades a few yards away! And many
of the junior officers, the subalterns and lieutenants, showed
no more courage than the raw recruits! To the veteran of
years of campaigning, this was the ultimate disgrace—that
officers who had been engaged to lead had become leaders
of a disorganized rout.

Thinking that perhaps daylight might bring a measure of
courage to his troops, Montgomery decided to wait until
morning, then to try once more to encircle the fort with
siege posts. But even then, after the sun's light showed them

that the night shadows had been only the hobgoblins of childish imagination, the men behaved no better. They started out, then ran back like frightened rabbits when someone cried out that the regulars were advancing on them. For the second time, Montgomery reluctantly ordered a retreat to the Ile aux Noix, where he wrote once more to Janet of his discouragement over the quality of his army:

> "Such a set of pusillanimous wretches never were collected! Could I, with decency, leave the army in its present situation, I would not serve an hour longer. I am much afraid the general character of the people has been too justly represented. However, there are some whose spirit I have confidence in. They are taking pains with the men, and they flatter me with hopes of prevailing upon them to retrieve their characters. . . .
>
> "Show this to your father only. It can't be of service to our common cause to publish our weakness. May I have better news to write hereafter! Adieu, my dearest Janet. Believe me most affectionately yours,
>
> *Richard Montgomery"*

For a full week the general worked night and day to prepare everything for a new advance on St. John's, one that must not fail. The boom across the river was completed, while boats and supplies were readied for the offensive push. This time only a small force would hold the fort by the boom; every other able-bodied man would move north to surround Fort St. John's and take it.

Now there was no avoidance of the showdown over military discipline that Montgomery had been postponing for weeks. A man of severe personal discipline himself by character and by training, he recognized that he was perhaps impatient with others who had not had his schooling at arms.

Yet he realized that this entire expeditionary force would fail unless he could quickly whip the laggards and cowards from it, and inspire his men and officers with a sense of their duty. Ordinary men become soldiers only when they learn to face shot and shell without faltering. Montgomery had to give them a soldier's confidence, stiffen their courage, build up their pride, instill in them a sense of purpose so high that they would stand and fight.

Almost every day the troops were mustered to hear lectures on the reasons for the expedition into Canada, and the nobility of the cause in which they had engaged. Hope was held out that if they could sweep on to Montreal in short order, they might be home well before their six-months' enlistment period was over, at the turn of the year. Miscreants were punished as an expample to others. Montgomery's orderly book recorded one court martial after another:

James Barry sentenced to thirty-nine lashes with the cat-o'-nine-tails for firing on Lieutenant Houston; Patrick Fay sentenced to menial fatigue duties for "running away, supposing he was pursued by the enemy, and throwing away his firelock"; Humphrey Hopkins fined twenty shillings of New York money for robbing Colonel Waterbury's store of rum; several men confined for "mutinous acts." Men were impressed with their responsibility for equipment. The indolent were warned that they must use the toilet holes, and not dirty the camp area. All men were charged not to fire their weapons except under orders, and only at the enemy.

By September 17th, Montgomery had cleared his camp of several hundred of the most worthless, lazy and ill men, whom he sent back to Fort Ticonderoga where General Schuyler could dispose of them as he saw fit. Embarking once again for the approach to St. John's, the general must have sensed that this third time he would have to succeed, or the entire expedition would fail.

Already he had detached two small parties, one under Colonel Ethan Allen and the other commanded by Major John Brown, sending them ahead to scout through the country north of St. John's to gauge the feelings of the Canadians toward the invasion force. Allen and Brown were both resourceful, courageous leaders, who knew how to travel light and fast through the countryside, and to defend themselves if need be. Both parties moved freely, without meeting resistance, because the British regulars were concentrated behind the defenses of Fort St. John's, and many Canadians warned the Americans of every movement of British troops in the vicinity. Both Allen and Brown had sent back word to Montgomery that the country north of St. John's and west to Montreal lay wide open to the colonial force. The Canadians were friendly, they reported, and the British forces were restricted to Fort Chambly, St. John's and the town of Montreal.

Toward evening of the seventeenth, Montgomery landed close to one thousand men just beyond cannon range upstream from the fort and established his base camp. Waiting until morning, the general set out himself at the head of five hundred men, and marched around St. John's to the west, following the same route along which his men had twice before fled in panic. Arriving at the Chambly road north of St. John's, the Americans came suddenly upon a party of the king's troops, equipped with several pieces of field artillery. Just a few hours before these regulars had beaten off an attack by Major Brown's force of about fifty men, which had struck this outer position prematurely, before Montgomery could hit the British from the west flank.

Taken by surprise, the regulars fired on the Americans for several minutes, though without doing much damage. Then, to Montgomery's tremendous joy, they fled hurriedly back to the safety of Fort St. John's.

At last, his unseasoned troops had seen the redcoats turn and run! This was a great boost for their morale, and Montgomery was elated. After directing his assault force in spreading out so as to hold the fort in view, and preparing to resist any possible attack from that quarter, the young commander returned to his base camp and penned a hasty though optimistic dispatch to Schuyler:

"The enemy, after an ill directed fire for some minutes, retired with precipitation. And lucky for them they did. For had we known their situation, which the thickness of woods prevented our finding out till it was too late, there would not a man of them have returned."

But there were drawbacks, Montgomery reported to his superior. The troops were still too ready to believe rumors that frightened them—for instance, that they had been lured under the guns of the fort, which would slaughter them with cross fire. Montgomery found the woodsmen from New Hampshire and Vermont were not yet as expert at forming into battle positions as he had hoped, and too many of them had hung back when they should have pressed on. Otherwise, Montgomery wrote to Schuyler, things were in good order. He had stationed five hundred men under Colonel Bedel at the road junction north of St. John's, and they were already at work with their entrenching tools building earthworks for a siege. Allen was at the town of Chambly, close to the fort of that name, enlisting Canadians into the colonial forces. And, best of all—on the night of the seventeenth Major Brown had seized eight carts heading for St. John's,

full of British army rum and gun carriages. He had the fore-
sight to hide them in the woods, and the British troops had
failed to recover them after beating off Brown's attack the
next morning.

The big need now was for money. It must be gold and
silver money, Schuyler was informed, because the Canadians would not accept paper currency issued by the other
colonies. Now that his army controlled most of the countryside, Montgomery believed, a supply of sound coins would
allow him to buy supplies from the friendly villagers and
farmers hereabouts.

Montgomery's satisfaction over beating the regulars in a
skirmish was increased a few hours later when a delegation
of seven chiefs of the Caghnawaga Indians appeared in
camp. Speaking through a half-breed interpreter, each in
turn assured the general of the peaceful intentions of their
people. A splendid belt of leather and beads was handed to
Montgomery as a symbol of their friendship. They bore no
grudge, the chiefs assured the American leader, over the
death of a few of their men who were killed in the fight on
September 6th. The colonists could not avoid firing back
when they were attacked.

Then the chiefs came to the real point of their visit. If the
general should take Fort St. John's, would he be magnani-
mous and release any Caghnawagas who might happen to be
within the fort? The general, they continued, must understand that the British had for months been spreading tales
among the Indians that the colonists from New York had
designs to seize their hunting grounds and to prevent their
practicing their own religion. Some of their people believed
these lies of the redcoats, the chiefs said gravely.

When he rose to reply to the circle of chiefs and officers,

Montgomery must have realized that the Indians were asking him for very little. Understanding and generosity on his part now might assure a friendly neutrality not only from this small group of Indians, but also from the other Indian nations in the province of Quebec. He was very happy that the chiefs had called on him, he said, and would immediately release any Caghnawagas who were among his prisoners. As to their brothers within the fort, Montgomery promised that if Providence should bless the invaders' arms with success and they should take Fort St. John's, not a hair on the head of any of their people found alive within it would be harmed. Furthermore, his men would avoid entering any of the Indians' camps, as the chiefs requested, so as not to frighten their women. Montgomery then went further, to the reason for the expedition. Because his own people were fighting for liberty and justice against ministerial tyranny, he said, they would never desire to molest the Indians or bring injustice to them. He begged the chiefs to inform the other Indian nations of this, and influence them to remain neutral in the colonists' war against the troops of the British ministry.

A present of four hundred pounds in New York currency solemnly passed to the chiefs as a sign of friendship, and to help them dry their tears over their dead people, brought the conference to a close. The Caghnawaga chiefs disappeared into the forest as silently as they had come, and Richard Montgomery turned now to the siege of Fort St. John's.

The layout of the fort was no secret to the Americans, because a number of the colonists had visited it in May, shortly after the seizure of Ticonderoga from the British, and before General Carleton had sent Major Charles Preston to garrison St. John's. In fact, while Benedict Arnold and Ethan Allen had been looking about for ways to display their military zeal before the invasion of Canada had been decided upon, both men determined to probe the British forts strung along the Sorel River. Arnold had moved first. Early on the morning of May 18th he descended on St. John's, overpowered the dozen soldiers that made up its skeleton force, and withdrew with a load of supplies, a captured sloop and twelve prisoners. Allen arrived a day later, only to find that his rival had beaten him to the prize. He retreated quickly when farmers near the fort told him that Major Preston with nearly one hundred fifty regulars was marching fast for St. John's.

Since Preston's arrival the British fort, situated on the ruins of the old French post, had been rebuilt into a strong redoubt measuring two hundred by two hundred fifty feet, with thick earth parapets. About six hundred feet north along the river bank Preston had his men erect a somewhat larger rectangular fortification, enclosing two houses and several outbuildings. Between the two redoubts ran a communications ditch, and on the river side were slips where the boats were built. The entire area was enclosed by a stout log stockade. By the time Montgomery closed the ring around this fortified place, Major Preston had under his command close to four hundred regular soldiers and more than one hundred Canadians and Indians. The garrison had been toiling all summer long to put St. John's in a posture for defense. Preston had adequate cannon and mortars at his disposal, plenty of ammunition, and a fair supply of food. Water flowed freely at the Sorel. But he was burdened by a hundred or more women and other refugees from the nearby country, who sought the protection of the fort from

fear that the Americans were an army of murderous looters.
All told there were nearly seven hundred people within its
walls.

Moving forward to reconnoitre the fort through the
woods near the river bank, Montgomery chose a point about
five hundred yards south of the near redoubt for a battery
of mortars. Closer than this his men would be visible, directly under the guns of the fort, because Preston had taken
the precaution to cut the brush and level buildings that
would offer concealment or protection. The siege of this
place, it was clear, would require all the artillery strength
that the Americans could bring forward.

Gun for gun, Preston enjoyed the advantage, since he had
two 8-inch howitzers, eight mortars, and more than thirty
cannon, among which were a pair of brass 24-pounders. But
Montgomery had the advantage of position. His force was
so widely dispersed that the British firepower could not
destroy it. On the other hand, the attacker's mortars and
cannon could hardly miss their target, and the dual fort was
so tightly pressed that almost every American shot was
bound to do damage to men, buildings or arms. The real
question was whether Fort St. John's could hold out one
week, or perhaps two, or even three before it would be
softened up for an infantry assault.

Montgomery positioned one battery of four guns on the
far side of the river just beyond a protective fringe of trees,
with a carry of about seven hundred yards to the target.
Another four-gun battery was placed west of the fort at
about the same distance, whereas the mortar battery was
placed within five hundred yards of the southern redoubt.

As both sides settled down to an exchange of shot and
shell, the chill rains of the northern equinox began to fall,

and kept up, with only slight intermissions, day after day. The entire battle area soon turned into a sticky quagmire. Black mud lay thick on every pathway, around every gun position, and over the tenting grounds. The men had to move their tents almost daily. They spread pine and hemlock boughs to ward off the damp chill of the mucky ground, but the cold of the Canadian autumn nevertheless penetrated to their bones. Campfires, which sent up telltale smoke, were allowed only beyond the range of the fort guns, and here each man when off duty could try to dry his clothing, after a fashion. But within a short while after a soldier had reached a pleasurable state of dryness and warmth at the fire, the cold rain and mud would soak his garments through again.

Every day and night guards stationed at a ring of outposts watched the fort, to prevent a possible surprise attack. Most of the men not on guard were busy digging redoubts of heavy earth to protect the mortarmen and gunners from the fire aimed at them from the fort. On the night of September 22nd, Montgomery sent Captain Samuel Mott, a Connecticut man assigned to the first New York regiment, to occupy the mortar redoubt and protect it while the work continued. Dark had fallen long since, when Montgomery at the base camp heard musket firing to the north. A little later the big guns of the fort boomed several times, followed by the explosion of enemy shells a bit too close for comfort. Then all was silent for a time. About nine o'clock the camp was stirred by voices coming from the direction of the mortar redoubt, and stragglers from Mott's party arrived in disorder. The mortar position, they declared, had been taken by the enemy.

Montgomery was astounded a few moments later to see

Captain Mott himself emerge from the woods. The captain reported that he had been at the redoubt when he had seen a party of regulars, perhaps one or two hundred, marching toward him. He could not make out their numbers for sure because it was so dark. He had hailed them, had received no answer, but was certain that he heard their officer cry out:

"March on, my boys!"

At this point, Mott declared, his own men fired one volley, then fled from the redoubt in a panic, despite his best efforts to halt them. The regulars, he added, had rushed into the position and he had only barely escaped himself.

Not long afterward, Montgomery heard another account of Captain Mott's brush with the enemy that put it in an entirely different light. One of Mott's lieutenants, who had been a slight distance from the redoubt, reported that he had heard that Mott's men were retreating in disorder. He told Montgomery he had thought it prudent to see if he could recover the working tools that the men had abandoned. Moving cautiously toward the redoubt with a squad of soldiers, he found the place utterly deserted. There was no sign of an enemy attack, the lieutenant added, and he believed there had not been one. Here were the picks and mattocks to prove his story.

Enraged almost beyond control at this report of Mott's cowardice, Montgomery sent another officer to occupy the redoubt and continue the work. When word reached him that the place was indeed empty of men, with no enemy anywhere in sight, Montgomery ordered Captain Mott put under arrest, and promised that he would be tried by court martial for shamefully deserting a post that he was ordered to maintain. In his own opinion, as Montgomery wrote in a dispatch to General Schuyler, the man deserved the firing squad if convicted by a court martial. But it was doubtful if a court of Mott's fellow-officers would condemn him to so severe a penalty.

Montgomery did not know at the time that Mott had been a secret voice of discontent and a troublemaker within his camp. He had been writing letters to Governor Trumbull of Connecticut complaining about virtually everything—the food, equipment, the army's lack of discipline and training—but above all, the rascality of the New Yorkers, as opposed to the Connecticut men. It looked as if he were trying to stir up ill feeling between the volunteers from the two colonies, when friction among them would only hinder the development of a united Continental army. In an expedition where almost everything seemed to go wrong, and every day brought its frustration and hardship, men from isolated farms and small villages who had seen very little of the rest of the country were easily persuaded that the fellows from the "other" colony were responsible for their troubles.

As Mott nursed his grievances against Montgomery and the New Yorkers while in confinement on board one of the river vessels, the general started a systematic bombardment of the fort. Every few nights one or two civilians would slip out from St. John's to escape the danger and discomfort of the siege. When questioned they said the American shots were striking home and doing grievous damage. Several buildings in the fort were half in ruins. Major Preston, according to some of these reports, after a week of artillery fire, had less ammunition and food than Montgomery had reckoned at first. Perhaps he could be brought to surrender without an infantry attack. His breastworks and pickets were strong, but his defenses were really only as stout as the hearts of his soldiers and officers. The wounded were suffering greatly, and many soldiers and civilian refugees were weak from fevers. When their will to resist would flag, the Americans could take St. John's.

Still the rains came down. Nights now brought frost, and by morning a skim of ice covered the wet places. It was not cold enough to freeze hard, but rather just enough to make the men thoroughly miserable in their soaked clothing and footgear. By day most of the men could be kept active improving their bivouac areas and digging new artillery positions. The mortars and guns were moved about several times as one wet day and night succeeded another, and each artillery position became a deeper nest of oozing muck, in which the guns would not hold firm.

Late in September Major Brown sent good news from La Prairie, near Montreal. To top his earlier seizure of British rum, he had now taken a large British army magazine of ammunition and food stores. About the time Montgomery received most of this haul, General Schuyler sent him a most welcome present from Ticonderoga—a heavy brass mortar with a bore 13 inches in diameter. The British had captured this prize from the French in the previous war, and because of the size and weight named it the "Old Sow." With this weapon Montgomery could lob his heaviest shot high over the earthwork defenses of Fort St. John's and drop them directly on the buildings inside. This was a bombardment where high-trajectory mortars and howitzers were doing most of the damage. His light cannon, which would carry farther, in most instances just sent their iron shot thudding into the packed earth of the breastworks. None of his gunners were experts at aiming and they had little practice by which to learn the peculiarities of their guns.

By the morning of September 28th, Montgomery could

report to General Schuyler that two of his 12-pound guns had opened fire on the British shipyard and schooner, and that the defenders had withdrawn the ship as far as they could toward the north end of the fort. The day before he had resolved to load a few cannon and the necessary ammunition onto flatboats and to send them downstream at night, directly past the fort and the St. John's rapids nearby. If the daring group of volunteers who would pilot them down this dangerous passage could get through, the guns could be used against the stone walls of Fort Chambly while he was besieging St. John's. Over a full week one raft followed another past fort and rapids, and not long thereafter the general heard that every shipment had landed safely near Chambly, where the British garrison was thought to be extremely small —perhaps just a few dozen men.

By this time both sides had tried one another's strength, and each knew his limits. The regulars were pinned down in their forts, while the Americans could march freely about the countryside, thanks to the friendly attitude of the Canadians. But one American officer miscalculated badly. He was the irrepressible Ethan Allen, who was made so bold by his liberty to move about the farm country between the Sorel and the St. Lawrence River that he thought all Canada would rally to him, wherever he went. Early on the morning of September 24th, he set out with thirty American soldiers and about fifty Canadian volunteers to cross the St. Lawrence and capture the town of Montreal. Allen thought that the townspeople would support him, and would not permit the small garrison commanded by Governor Carleton and General Prescott to put up a fight.

But he was dead wrong. Allen was not on the far shore more than a couple of hours before his small force was completely surrounded and overwhelmed by a mixed band of regulars and Canadian militiamen who had rallied to the British flag to defend their town. After two hours of wall-and-hedge firing and running, Allen surrendered to spare the lives of his little band of followers. Taken before Prescott, he was identified as the rebel who had seized Fort Ticonderoga to the great embarrassment of the king's forces. By nightfall Allen was lying in a cold prison, his ankles shackled to a heavy iron bar, and his wrists bound in chains. Four days later Montgomery learned from several witnesses the result to which Allen's vanity had led.

"I have to lament Mr. Allen's imprudence and ambition," Montgomery wrote to General Schuyler, "which urged him to this affair singlehanded, when he might have had a considerable reinforcement."

Early in October whisperings reached the general's ears of mutinous talk among the junior officers. They were sick of the campaign, distressed at the discomfort of this cold, damp Canadian swamp in which they were living like half-drowned rats. Mott had stirred a number of them to speaking up in his behalf, as though he were the victim of injustice from a tyrannical, half-mad young general. Montgomery tried to appear confident, but he was expecting many officers to quit any day.

Then suddenly the skies cleared, and the camp before St. John's was cheered by the bright sun of early autumn. Several large shipments of pork, flour, sugar and gunpowder came through from Fort Ticonderoga. General Schuyler's repeated calls upon General Washington, on the New York Congress and on the Continental Congress were being answered at last. And nearly a thousand more men were on the way under General David Wooster, who had agreed to put himself under General Montgomery even though he was Montgomery's senior in age and service in the American colonies. These few events somehow changed the entire atmosphere in the American camp, and morale rose rapidly. Talk of mutiny subsided, and the general released Captain Mott and all other men under detention for breaches of discipline.

The siege was nearly four weeks old on October 13th, when Montgomery called his ranking officers into a council of war. Patiently he explained that the best hope of smashing the St. John's defenses and taking the fort lay in moving the batteries around to the high ground on the northwest. From a small hill within four hundred yards of the north fort they could pour in fire before the British could move their defense guns around to strike back. Then they could storm into the breach if a demand for surrender were not accepted.

But the general found almost no support among his council. To a man, his field officers preferred to fire at the fort from a safe position across the Sorel River, even at the risk of permitting the entire garrison to escape to La Prairie and thence to Montreal. They wanted to be safe themselves, and not risk an infantry battle. Reluctantly, Montgomery had to recognize that he must compromise. If his colonels, majors and captains would not accept his strategy, he had no power to force his will on them. The discipline of the British army was unknown to these gentlemen volunteers, who were free to resign pretty much as they willed.

Eventually, it was decided to split the artillery. Some pieces were ferried across the stream and aimed at the fort from the east, while a few others were left in the old battery positions facing the south fort. Meanwhile, with the increase

in ammunition and more guns sent forward from Ticonderoga, the midnight runs downstream toward Chambly
continued. By day the American batteries pounded the fort
and the British vessels with heavy shot and with red-hot bits
of small iron to spread fire amid their sails and rigging.
Smoke hung heavy over St. John's and the Sorel as the guns
flashed and boomed intermittently from both fort and the
surrounding woods. By the seventeenth the Americans could
tell from the way the schooner was listing heavily to one side
that she had been severely wounded, and could not threaten
the lake this season.

On October 19th a breathless courier from Major Brown
ran into camp to bring the most startling and welcome news
of the campaign. Fort Chambly had capitulated! That old
French strongpoint, with its massive stone walls built to
withstand the heaviest cannonading, had been handed over
to Brown by a timorous commandant, a Major James Stopford of the Royal Fusiliers, after only a few shots had been
fired. True, Stopford had only ninety regular soldiers and
officers to defend the place, but his walls were high and solid.
He could very easily have held Brown at bay for several
weeks, if he had had any kind of fighting heart. But Stopford was a weakling, with none of the iron in his character
that Major Preston was displaying at Fort St. John's.

Although Brown was in command, the force that took
Fort Chambly was composed largely of Canadian volunteers, and indeed the entire attack plan of sending the
artillery down the rapids by night had been proposed to
Montgomery by Canadian allies who knew the Sorel River
currents. When the Fort Chambly storehouses were opened,
they were found to be stocked with all the ammunition and
food required to finish the reduction of Fort St. John's. Six

tons of gunpowder, cannon shot, musket shot, sixty-five hundred musket cartridges, five hundred hand grenades and one hundred fifty French rifles were among the military stores. As for food, the Americans hauled out eighty barrels of flour, one hundred and thirty-four barrels of pork, and large quantities of rice, peas and butter. Of special value as a souvenir of their victory, the Americans carried into camp the colors of the British Seventh Regiment. In a dispatch to General Schuyler on the wonderful turn in their fortunes, Montgomery praised Brown and his Canadian comrades, and showed that he now looked on the campaign with optimism:

"The enemy's schooner is sunk. They have not been very anxious to save her, else they might easily have protracted her fate. I must now think that unless some unlucky accident befalls us, we shall accomplish our business here, and I shall set to work in earnest on this side of the water. The troops are in high spirits." Then, alluding to the one item, always in short supply, that warmed the soldiers in body and heart, he pleaded with Schuyler:

"Let us have rum, my dear General, else we shall never be able to go through our business."

With Major Stopford's surrender, close to a hundred women and children belonging to the families of his men and officers fell into Montgomery's hands. A day's truce was arranged with Major Preston at Fort St. John's, during which the dependents were allowed to pass upstream by boats under the guns of the fort and of the besiegers. Montgomery thought that the sight of these helpless civilians as well as the military prisoners taken at Chambly would help to undermine the will to resist in St. John's.

Although the prisoners were a burden to his army, they

could be useful in arranging better treatment for Americans, such as Allen, who had fallen into enemy hands. In a message sent by courier to Governor Carleton in Montreal, Montgomery protested the inhumanity of Carleton's keeping Allen in irons, and pointed out his "most painful reluctance" to retaliate by treating Major Stopford and others in like manner. Appealing to Carleton as one Englishman to another, Montgomery begged that the present dispute among British subjects not sink to a level of inhumanity improper even in war with foreigners, and concluded:

"I shall expect your excellency's answer in six days. Should the bearer not return in that time, I must interpret your silence into a declaration of barbarous war.

"I cannot pass this opportunity without lamenting the melancholy and fatal necessity which obliges the firmest friends of the Constitution to oppose one of the most respectable officers of the Crown."

Guy Carleton, fourteen years older than Montgomery, was no stranger to the commander of the American expeditionary force. He was a career officer known as the best trained military engineer in the British army. As a colonel in 1759, Carleton had been one of the most trusted advisers to General James Wolfe during the war against the French, and was with him that fateful day on the Plains of Abraham, before Quebec. Montgomery had seen Carleton's star rise with the conquest of Canada, and knew that as Governor-General of Canada and commander of the king's forces in the province, Carleton would be proud and hard in dealing with a junior of many years whom he considered nothing more than an upstart and a rebel.

General Carleton let word filter back to Montgomery from Montreal that he would not even consider his message

—as if to make the younger man feel his disdain. But Carleton's military strength was not the equal of his pride and his posture as the king's representative in Quebec Province. Aware that the fall of Chambly would lead to the doom of Fort St. John's unless he came to its relief, Carleton raised every man in Montreal whom he could round up to bear a musket, and set off in boats to cross the St. Lawrence and march to the relief of Major Preston. It was a bold act by a desperate and courageous officer, but it was futile. Roughly five hundred armed Americans and Canadian volunteers were lined along the shore opposite Montreal, where they had been waiting and watching for a month since the defeat of Ethan Allen. Carleton's force was beaten back after a furious battle of musket-fire. By evening of October 31st, Major Preston and his garrison knew that with Carleton's failure their position was hopeless. Nevertheless, his soldier's pride would not allow him to raise the white flag while he still had some capacity to resist.

On the morning of November 1st, Montgomery's batteries opened up on St. John's with every available barrel, and kept firing as rapidly as the guns could be cooled, swabbed and reloaded. From his forward position with his spyglass Montgomery could discern the shattering effect of his fire on the roofs and walls of the buildings in view. From within the twin forts as the long day wore on, the reply shots became ever less frequent. It was obvious now that Montgomery had been correctly informed by refugees who had escaped the fort. Preston's ammunition, after six weeks of siege, was running very low. Part of his force was dead, or near death from their wounds. Those of his men who were still on their feet were deadly weary from lack of sleep, and weak from hunger and fevers.

Toward evening Montgomery ordered a halt in the cannonade and sent an officer under a flag of truce to demand the surrender of the garrison. Preston, in reply, sent Montgomery a letter saying that he was equally anxious to prevent the further spilling of blood and "to maintain the honor of His Majesty's arms." He proposed that he would hold out another four days. If, after that, no relief should reach him, he would then offer Montgomery his proposals for surrender.

Now, Montgomery realized, his opponent could be pressed to capitulate. But four days' time was too high a price to pay to the beaten garrison for the sake of their honor. Major Charles Preston of the 26th Regiment, all credit to his efforts in the wrong cause, had held up the American campaign far too long already. Quebec must be cleared of the British forces before winter would close down over this entire country.

"The advanced season of the year will not admit of your proposal," Montgomery wrote back immediately to Preston. "Having now acquitted my conscience, I must, to save time and prevent trouble, acquaint you, if you do not surrender this day, it will be unnecessary to make any future proposals." If fighting should resume, Montgomery said, the entire garrison would be prisoners of war without the customary courtesies and honors of war. This would mean, among other things, that the officers would not be guaranteed their personal baggage.

"Should you still be inclined to persist in a useless defense, you will immediately fire a cannon without shot, as a signal."

Darkness had fallen by the time Montgomery's message was written, and it was not delivered to the fort until dawn, after a night of anxious stillness at the batteries. By mid-morning a jubilant cry swept through the American camp, from one battery and outpost to another:

"Victory!"

[The fort was capitulating! The white fag was flying over St. John's! After forty-five days and nights of siege, the battle was over.]

Most of the day was busily filled with preparing and copying the terms of capitulation at headquarters, while exhausted, disheartened defenders on the one side gathered their gear in preparation for surrender as prisoners of war. On the other side, the American officers hurried to dress up their camp, to force the men to wash, shave, wipe the mud from their weapons, and somehow do their best to look like a victorious army. By late afternoon the details for surrender of the garrison had been agreed to, and signatures of both Major Charles Preston and General Richard Montgomery had been affixed.

The following morning, as agreed, the garrison troops and officers totaling some seven hundred men marched out from Fort St. John's with the honors of war—flags flying, drums beating, and arms in hand. The soldiers grounded their arms for collection by the victors, and then boarded the waiting boats for transport back to Connecticut colony. Eventually they were to be conducted to General Gage, the British commander in Boston, for shipment back to England. The officers were sent with their men, but were permitted to retain their side-arms. Every man was allowed to keep his blankets, clothing and baggage. Montgomery would have no plundering of anyone's personal property.

The surrender ceremony over, Montgomery's supply offi-

cers quickly surveyed the military stores yielded by the conquered fort, to find what could be useful in moving the army
on to Montreal, and thence down the St. Lawrence River
valley to clear it of British troops. The prize of battle included two heavy brass cannon, 24-pounders, nineteen
smaller brass cannon and howitzers, twenty-two iron cannon,
mostly 9-pounders and 6-pounders, and a few mortars. Of
equal importance were the naval stores, which would be
vital in controlling the rivers on the Quebec side of the
border, and the lakes on the New York side. The St. John's
shipyard yielded a large stock of cables, ropes, anchors,
sails and sailcloth, nails and spikes, pitch, tar, linseed oil,
iron kettles and tallow. Indeed, the Americans now had their
own well-stocked shipyard.

The surrender of St. John's had come none too soon. As
Montgomery broke camp and marched northwest toward
Montreal, he knew that Major Preston's stubborn resistance
on the Sorel had cost him dearly. Were he on this road four
or five weeks earlier—if it were now the beginning of October instead of November—things might have been much
more favorable. His men had spent a miserable autumn in
the wet and cold before St. John's, without adequate shelter.
A scant two or three dozen of his men had been killed by
gunfire in the campaign so far, or had died of wounds. But
nearly one thousand had been sent back because of illness,
or because they were such useless, undisciplined wretches
that the army was better off without them. Now, with about
fourteen hundred men in his command, he would cross the
broad St. Lawrence and attack Montreal.

Would General Carleton stand and fight, as Major Preston had done? Or would he retreat downstream, and defy

pursuit? The next few days would tell. But whatever course he would choose, Carleton would maneuver and fight with all the craftiness of an experienced old fox. For Montgomery knew that he was now face to face with the most resourceful, capable general officer in the British army.

❀ 6 ❀

One Square Mile of Canada

ALMOST as if the capture of St. John's were a signal to the elements, the Canadian winter descended upon the Americans as they were gathering in the booty from the fallen fort. A stinging, wet snow, whipped by a raw wind, fell on bare faces and hands, and plastered the men's rough clothing in grotesque, soggy lumps. By the time Montgomery's column had started the twenty-mile journey toward La Prairie, which lay on the St. Lawrence opposite Montreal, everyone was eager to find shelter in town. A barn filled with hay would do as well as a mansion for most of the soldiers, who had lived outdoors for many weeks in cold, rain and mud.

General Montgomery's greatest concern was to move his newly captured artillery pieces and ammunition overland as rapidly as possible. The cannon and mortars could be used to overawe Montreal and force a quick surrender. Very soon the St. Lawrence would be so full of ice that he could not venture to cross in small boats. And he did not dare wait until the broad river should freeze solid, for by that time his army might melt away through illness and desertions. During the better part of a week, therefore, the general pushed and pleaded, goaded and flattered, in order to move his army and weapons across the muddy plain without losing any more valuable time. Already Fort St. John's had cost him several valuable autumn weeks—for which he could partly blame the weakness of his own army, but perhaps more Major Preston's stubborn defense.

Now, however, that he was face to face with General Guy Carleton, Montgomery had to plan on a much more ambitious scale than in the limited campaign against the fort. His objective was the entire St. Lawrence Valley. Only in the past few days had he felt free to reveal to his most trusted officers General Washington's grand strategy for the invasion of Canada, of which this army now facing Montreal was but one part. A second column of American soldiers, he told them, was approaching Quebec City, 150 miles to the northeast. Or they might even now be in possession of that old fortress town, the capital of the province.

The plan to send a secret invasion force to Quebec had matured in midsummer at General Washington's headquarters in Cambridge. Schuyler and Montgomery had been putting their force together for the main thrust straight northward from New York, when Benedict Arnold left Ticonderoga and suddenly presented himself to George Washington. Why wait for a big army to be organized and equipped and moved slowly?—Arnold asked the commander in chief. Why not send a smaller, light-armed party of tough backwoodsmen through the wilderness of Maine, to strike directly at Quebec City while the British were massing to meet Schuyler on the lakes and near Montreal?

Arnold, with a career of trading as his background, was

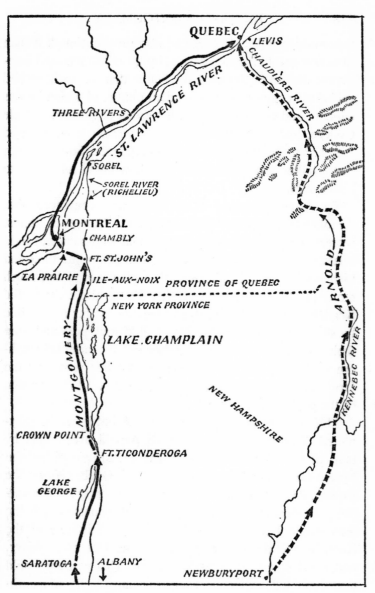

INVASION ROUTES TO QUEBEC

a persuasive talker. But he had also proved himself a man of action and of intrepid daring, by his bold raids on Ticonderoga and on St. John's. Even before that, in April, he had rallied his company of Connecticut militia, of which he was captain, and augmenting it with a group of students at Yale College, had seized the New Haven powder magazine and marched to Cambridge, armed and equipped. So he was not just a talker, but a doer, who somehow could rally men to follow him.

By August General Washington was convinced that Arnold's scheme made sense. Under the blanket of utmost secrecy, he arranged to provide Arnold with sufficient light boats, powder, shot and food stores to equip one thousand men, mostly New Englanders. The plan was to sail north along the Massachusetts and New Hampshire coast to the Kennebec River, then proceed upstream as far as possible by ship. From here on the men would row, pole and drag their small boats, following the river into the unsettled northern wilderness that lay between the Atlantic coast and the farm country in the province of Quebec, on the near side of the capital city.

This territory was wild and unsettled, but it had been explored. Washington conferred with Arnold over a sketchy map of the district, drawn by the British engineer John Montresor, following the conquest of Quebec from the French. Arnold's force was to concentrate on speed and surprise. Its heaviest burdens would be the boats, which the men would have to portage from the headwaters of the Kennebec to the upper reaches of the Chaudière River, which led down to the St. Lawrence. This journey would lead through dense woods, where they must hack out a pathway wide enough for them to stagger with boats and stores.

Traders, hunters and Indians alone had been along this route. But if they had managed it, Arnold felt confident that he could lead an army on the same path.

As Montgomery left St. John's for Montreal, he still had no word of Arnold's arrival near Quebec. The last messages had come through long before, having been sent back from Arnold in early October when he was desperately pushing through the wooded, boggy wilderness between the head-waters of the Kennebec and the Chaudière rivers. His men were ragged, hungry and terribly worn by their ordeal, having no carts and horses, and therefore being forced to move all the equipment of an army on their own backs. Several hundred men had been lost through illness and desertion, and a few had died. But that was the last word from Arnold, relayed all the way in a great circle back down the Kennebec to Cambridge, then overland to Schuyler at Ticonderoga, and thence by messenger to Montgomery's camp before St. John's.

In the past month, Montgomery constantly asked himself, had Arnold pushed his men into Canada and was he now nearing Quebec? Or was he in possession of the city? Montgomery hoped for some days that every messenger arriving at his headquarters would bring news. For if Arnold now stood on the lower St. Lawrence with even five hundred men of his original force, then between them they might complete the business of clearing the regulars from the entire province.

As Montgomery's men warmed their bodies and dried their clothes in the houses and barns of La Prairie and surrounding villages, civilian messengers from Montreal were shuttling back and forth between the city and the invasion army headquarters. One after another, they reported that

General Carleton, after his failure in trying to relieve St. John's, had lost all control over the populace of Montreal. When he called for volunteers to defend the city against the invading "Bostonians," as the Canadians called the Americans, only a tiny handful responded.

Montreal was highly vulnerable to attack. The town was laid out in a long rectangle along the water's edge, with no outer defenses. It could be surrounded and starved by an enemy, and could be easily cut off from relief by ships. Or it could be stormed and taken at a number of points by perhaps five hundred men. The inhabitants, both French and English, had no reason to encourage the ruin of their town by bombardment, when they were certain it would be occupied in any event. The taking of St. John's by the Americans had proved that the invaders were far more powerful than Carleton and all the troops he could muster now. The merchants and householders of Montreal therefore were most anxious that Montgomery not make an artillery target of their town. And Montgomery, on his side, hoped to avoid a battle here.

Using his informants from Montreal as messengers, he sent an appeal to its inhabitants from his post on the southeast shore from which he could plainly see the stone walls and roofs of the old town, just three miles away under the shadow of Mount Royal, where Carleton's small flotilla of ships were drawn up at the piers.

"My anxiety for the fate of Montreal," Montgomery's message declared, "induces me to request that you will exert yourselves among the inhabitants to prevail on them to enter into such measures as will prevent the necessity of opening my batteries on the town."

Montgomery's appeal for surrender pointed to the "dreadful consequences of a bombardment," the suffering of the innocent and helpless, the menace of fire in winter. He urged them "to take every possible step to soften the heart of the Governor," and deter him from a futile resistance that would bring misery to the inhabitants and "lasting disgrace to his own humanity." Finally, Montgomery declared it had been "falsely and scandalously reported that our intentions are to plunder" in Montreal. The Americans, he declared, had not done so since entering the province, as every Canadian had observed.

Guy Carleton knew that he could not defend Montreal against Montgomery's army, because he had a scant 150 soldiers at his command. Even if he were to put up a defense around the walls of Montreal, as soon as firing should start, the discontented civilians would open the city to the American "rebels," as he termed them. But if he could retreat from Montreal by night, and sail down the St. Lawrence to Quebec, taking with him as much of the artillery and powder as he could stow quickly aboard the dozen vessels still at his disposal here, he might make a stand behind the thick walls of Quebec, where the terrain would favor the defense. Furthermore, Carleton counted on it that within the next few weeks winter would fix its icy grip on this part of the world, and these ill-supplied invaders might lose half their men to the elements.

On November 11th, Montgomery moved forward, crossing the broadest part of the St. Lawrence with two regiments to St. Paul's Island, which lay close to the city. During the night a negotiating committee of twelve Montreal men of importance drafted articles of capitulation, which they delivered to Montgomery the next morning. Meanwhile, news came to the general that Carleton had slipped out of the

city during the long night, after having had his soldiers tem-
porarily disable the Montreal defense guns by driving an
iron spike tightly into the fire-hole of each cannon. With
him had gone General Prescott, about one hundred thirty
regular troops who were physically fit, and eleven river vessels with their crews. Aboard the ships was most of the city's
store of gunpowder.

Disappointed that he had missed his opportunity to capture a pair of British generals with the town, Montgomery
nonetheless entered Montreal on the morning of November
13th at the head of his column, without the firing of a single
shot. A printer was found who immediately published a
large broadside which was posted conspicuously where the
inhabitants of Montreal could read, in both French and
English, the terms under which General Montgomery was
occupying their town and province.

The Continental army, having come for the purpose of
"giving liberty and security," the general said, there would
be no acts of oppression or violence. Property would be
secure, and religious liberty would be insured for all. Most
significant to these townsfolk was Montgomery's appeal to
all Canadians to join the other thirteen colonies in their
struggle against tyranny:

> "The General hopes to see such a virtuous Provin-
> cial Convention assembled as will enter with zeal into
> every measure that can contribute to set the civil and
> religious rights of this and her sister Colonies on a per-
> manent foundation. He promises, for himself, that he
> will not compel the inhabitants of the town to take up
> arms against the Mother Country, or contribute to-
> wards the expenses of carrying on the present war.
> "The Continental Army came into this Province for

its protection; they therefore cannot consider their opposers as taking up arms for its defense . . . Speedy measures shall be taken for establishing courts of justice upon the most liberal plan, conformable to the British Constitution."

Montreal had once been Montgomery's final objective, but it could not be any longer. Winter might indeed buy the Americans time. But they could not be secure from a British invasion in the spring unless the regulars were deprived of any fortifiable foothold in the province. And as long as Guy Carleton, that wily and resourceful old fox, was loose in this country, with men and guns sufficient to protect him from capture, New England could not be safe. Montreal must therefore be looked on now as only a staging area. The war must be carried down the St. Lawrence to Quebec.

As Montgomery's men were settling into comfortable quarters within the town, a courier brought news, at long last, from Benedict Arnold. With seven hundred men of his original thousand, he was at Levis, directly across the St. Lawrence River from fortress Quebec. He planned, Arnold wrote, to cross the broad body of water to the north shore just as soon as he had assembled enough boats and the river would be calm. His message told Montgomery of his long march, four hundred miles from the Maine coast, most of it through wilderness, where his men suffered seemingly endless agonies from weariness, hunger, injuries, fever and despair. Half a hundred fresh graves marked the path along which Arnold's expeditionary force had traveled since mid-September. Now, thanks to their remarkable fortitude, this body of men had it in their power to close the trap on General Guy Carleton, and so help end the war in Canada before the turn of the year.

In a mixed mood of perplexity and determination, Montgomery reported in detail to General Schuyler the first evening he was lodged in Montreal. Arnold was safely before Quebec. But as long as the British still held this fortress town, protected by massive walls and steep, rocky palisades, "this business," as he called the Canadian campaign, would remain unfinished. Montgomery wrote that he would join Arnold's force and besiege Quebec "if the severe season holds off, and I can prevail on the troops to accompany me."

That was the difficulty—getting the troops to leave the comforts of Montreal for the uncertainty of a winter campaign, when snow had already covered the ground and ice was forming in the St. Lawrence. He must be empowered to enlist men for an additional six months, Montgomery urged General Schuyler, or most of the troops would disappear at the end of December. When at St. John's he had even felt himself forced to coax the men on to Montreal by offering them the right to be discharged from service if only they would remain with him until Montreal were taken. Many were in a mood to go home now, Montgomery wrote. And though he felt sure that enough men would stay under arms to hold the American positions through the winter, they had to push the British army from all of Canada.

"It is of the utmost importance to finish this business at once, that the Ministry may have no hopes left of carrying on their infernal plan in this important quarter. At any rate, it will be highly expedient to throw in a large body of troops as soon as the ice will bear, in order to make a vigorous attack on Quebec before the arrival of succours in the spring, should it not fall into our hands this winter."

Again, as he had done frequently before in his dispatches, Montgomery told Schuyler that he was weary of war, and hoped that he could be relieved as soon as the Quebec campaign were won:

"I must go home, even if I walk by the side of the lake, this winter. I am weary of power, and totally want that patience and temper so requisite for such a command."

Then back again to his first concern, the lack of discipline among his command—officers as well as enlisted men—many of whom had no proper sense of duty or self-discipline. The officers of the First Regiment of Yorkers and the artillery company, Montgomery wrote, "were very near a mutiny" when he had insisted they could not loot the private clothing of the prisoners taken at St. John's:

"I would not have sullied my own reputation, nor disgraced the Continental arms, by such a breach of capitulation, for the universe. There was no driving it into their noddles that the clothing was really the property of the soldier, and that he had paid for it. . . . I wish some method could be fallen upon of engaging *gentlemen* to serve. A point of honor and more knowledge of the world, to be found in that class of men, would greatly reform discipline and render the troops much more tractable."

In spite of all his difficulties, however, Richard Montgomery recognized that he had been highly successful and lucky so far. Six months ago he had been nothing more than a gentleman farmer, a soldier in retirement who had been chosen to represent his county in the provincial assembly of New York. Now he was in faraway Montreal, at the head of an army that had sprung into being from virtually nothing. With it, he had driven the king's troops into retreat, had taken hundreds of prisoners, seized a powerful fort and occupied the second city of Quebec Province. Even now, two British army generals were fleeing his advance.

"I have courted Fortune and found her kind," Montgomery wrote to Robert Livingston from Montreal. "I have one more favor to solicit and then I have done . . . If the season remain favorable and the troops will follow me, I shall lend a hand to Arnold." And in like manner he wrote to Schuyler:

"My vexation and distress can only be alleviated by reflecting on the great public advantages which must arise from my unparalleled good fortune."

Although Montgomery could not have known it at the time, General Washington in Cambridge was on that very day rejoicing at the news of the capture of St. John's. In honor of the victory Washington ordered that the next day's password in his camp be "St. John's," and the countersign: "Montgomery." The commander in chief announced his hope that the members of his army "will show their gratitude to Providence for thus favoring the cause of freedom and America."

Two days after his entry into Montreal, Richard Montgomery summoned all the diplomacy and eloquence at his command in appealing to his army to follow him to Quebec. It was a strange position for an officer raised in the rigid professional discipline of British arms—but this was a strange kind of warfare. Montgomery was, in effect, a commander of men and officers whom he could not order against their will. Now that they were out of physical danger, were warmly housed in Montreal, and were being fed generously for the first time in months, none of them was eager to leave this haven for the cold and wet of a winter campaign.

They could not be whipped to it, for these colonists had

taken the spirit of liberty to heart and carried it with them as soldiers into the field. They were freemen and volunteers, not the subservient soldiery of Europe who bowed to the will of titled generals. Galling as it was to him as a military commander, Montgomery had learned, through frustrating weeks of campaigning, that he must endure a certain degree of mutinous insubordination from his officers and men. He must appeal to their better natures, to offer rewards and inducements rather than threaten punishments. Above all, he had to count on their patriotism and self-esteem to rally them for one final thrust against the enemy. The opening words of Montgomery's proclamation to the massed troops, read out on November 15th, must have caused him to swallow hard at his suppression of his true feelings:

"The General embraces this happy occasion of making his acknowledgments to the troops, for their patience and perseverance during the course of a fatiguing campaign. They have merited the applause of their grateful countrymen."

The promise made at St. John's would be honored, Montgomery continued. Those men who felt they must return home would be given passes, and furnished with boats and provisions for the journey. Yet he felt assured that most of the troops would stay with him, impelled by their "generous valor," by their "attachment to the interest of the United Colonies," and their "regard for their own honor." Every soldier engaging for the rest of the campaign would be paid one dollar bounty, and furnished with a winter outfit, including wool coat, vest, breeches, two shirts, stockings, shoes, winter mittens and cap. The troops were asked to engage only until April 15th of the following year. They would be discharged sooner if expected reinforcements arrived before that time. Montgomery declared that he—

"... entreats the troops not to lay him under the necessity of abandoning Canada, of undoing in one day what has been the work of months, and of restoring to an enraged and hitherto disappointed enemy the means of carrying a cruel war into the very bowels of their country. ... He has still hopes, notwithstanding the advanced season of the year, to reduce Quebec in conjunction with the troops which have penetrated by way of the Kennebec River, and thereby deprive the Ministerial Army of all footing in this important province."

To Montgomery's great relief, his proclamation brought the desired result. Most of the men and officers determined to remain in the army rather than quit. As each day passed the American troops in Montreal began to look more like healthy, well-equipped fighters prepared to oppose the winter elements as well as the enemy, in contrast to their ragged, ill-kept appearance during the siege of St. John's. Here and there a piece of British uniform red appeared on a Continental soldier, as enemy stores were distributed where needed. Large bundles of British uniforms, combined from garrison stocks taken at Chambly, St. John's and Montreal, were packed for transport to Arnold's men, who had left Massachusetts with nothing but their summer equipment.

The latest news from Arnold, which reached Montreal as Montgomery was re-forming his units and equipping them for winter, was ominous. The bold young colonel from Connecticut had gathered a small fleet of birchbark canoes, and by ferrying back and forth had taken five hundred men across the St. Lawrence from Levis. The crossing had taken place during the night of November 13th, Montgomery's first night within the walls of Montreal, and was accomplished by silently evading a number of heavily armed British patrol boats. Partly, perhaps, because of his theatrical nature, but more likely because the terrain dictated his course, Arnold followed almost the exact route taken by James Wolfe sixteen years before. He brought his men ashore at a small, sheltered cove which the French called the Anse du Foulon, but which the English since the conquest had termed Wolfe's Cove. Here, where a narrow, winding cleft in the rock cliffs had been cut by a stream, a steep path led upward to the Plains of Abraham at a point two miles west of the Quebec city walls. When a cold, gray dawn broke on November 14th, Arnold stood on the same high ground where the immortal Wolfe had been in 1759, and looked upon his prize—Fortress Quebec—which he had toiled over four hundred miles to attain. This town represented the one square mile in all Canada still under control of the British army.

Montgomery learned further from Arnold's dispatches that he had lost no time in sending an officer under a flag of truce toward the city gate, carrying with him Arnold's bold demand for the surrender of the city, in the name of General Washington and the Continental Congress. The demand was addressed to Hector Cramahé, the French Lieutenant-Governor of the province, in the absence of Governor-General Carleton. There was some reason for hope in the American camp that the sympathies of this predominantly French city would lie with the United Colonies rather that with the British army, its foe of just a few years past.

But Arnold had not yet learned that Colonel MacLean of the Royal Fusiliers, a retired soldier-of-fortune, had slipped into Quebec by boat the night before the Americans had crossed the St. Lawrence from Levis. With him MacLean brought three hundred British volunteers, gathered from all parts of the province. Among them were some sailors, a few marines, ex-servicemen immigrants and a few regulars. All of them were determined to fight here for their king and flag, and these men, not the French, now manned the walls of Quebec. They greeted Arnold's messenger with a burst of grapeshot and musket-fire that forced him to run for cover. Indignant over this treatment of his official representative, the proud Arnold the next day sent a message of protest to Cramahé, terming the attack "an insult I could not have expected from a private soldier, much less an officer of your rank." Again, the men under MacLean's command drove the messengers away with their fire.

Now, Arnold wrote to Montgomery, he must have assistance from the general. For while he had the men to patrol the villages around Quebec, and though the people in general were friendly, the city was defended in force. Furthermore his little army lacked the one essential for taking the town—artillery for a bombardment. He had brought with him only a few small field pieces that his men could wheel into position. But their light shot would have the same effect on Quebec's thick stone fortifications as a few apples that boys might throw against a brick wall. He needed more men, he required winter clothing for his half-naked troops, and he must have heavy-calibre guns. Until Montgomery should arrive, Arnold wrote, he would retire to a safe position at Point aux Trembles, a day's march upstream from Quebec City.

At some point between Arnold's camp and his present position in Montreal, Montgomery hoped to take General Carleton prisoner. General Prescott was a much less important figure in this war of maneuver, because he was the kind of unimaginative general whose course of action was almost completely predictable. Prescott was an old-fashioned officer, a despotic person who enjoyed the power of command. He relished comfort. He liked to lord it over both the military and the civilians in his control, ordering the best of quarters, food and liquors for himself whether his men were cared for or not.

Guy Carleton, on the other hand, was a man of intellect who thought far beyond himself. Now fifty-one, Carleton had started off with the advantages of money and education, having been born into a propertied family in Northern Ireland. But he owed his rise in the army to his keeness of mind and hard work. At age twenty-nine, it was his good fortune to be appointed military tutor to the Duke of Richmond, and in this post he traveled widely through Europe, making a special study of fortifications designed by such masters as the great French engineer Vauban. As a result he became a skilled tactician in the arts of defense and siege. In the early stages of the French war in Canada, Carleton fell into disfavor with the aged King George II, and was not permitted to accompany Generals Amherst and Wolfe in the assault on Louisbourg. Wolfe, who was his personal friend, thought so highly of Carleton's engineering skill that he wrote from Louisbourg in protest to one of the King's ministers:

"If his Majesty had thought proper to let Carleton come with us as engineer, it would cut the matter much shorter, and we might now be ruining the walls of Quebec and completing the conquest of New France."

The following year General Wolfe insisted that Carleton's aid was essential to his siege of Quebec, and Carleton was one of his right-hand men in the campaign until Wolfe died of his wounds before Quebec in the final battle with Montcalm. "All my books and papers, both here and in England, I leave to Colonel Carleton," Wolfe had written in his will, he further remembered his close friend with a bequest of one thousand pounds.

In the latter stages of the struggle with France, Carleton had served at Havana and other places where Richard Montgomery's path and his own crossed on occasion. There was, of course, a distance between them—the older man having the rank of colonel and later general, whereas young Montgomery served during the war as lieutenant and captain. But though they were not personally and intimately acquainted, Montgomery knew a great deal about Carleton's distinguished military record, his vast capabilities, his numerous battle wounds and his family connections in Ireland.

He knew, further, that General Carleton, after being named Governor of Quebec during the years of peace, had spent a great deal of time in Britain designing the Quebec Act, by which Parliament proposed to govern the province through relying on the old French landlord system and on the clergy. Governor-General Carleton was therefore the architect of the new regime in the province, announced just the year before, which was highly unpopular both with the post-war British immigrants in Canada and with the colonists elsewhere in North America. Though a man of great accomplishment, of learning, and of personal courage, the general was at the same time an enemy of colonial liberty.

Because Carleton was shrewd and resourceful, Montgomery knew that he would never be caught napping, like the stupid British commandant at Ticonderoga last May. Nor would he show the white feather, like Major Stopford at Chambly. Carleton had done his best to come to the aid of St. John's, and was beaten back by superior force. He had disabled most of the guns in Montreal, carried off much of the gunpowder, and eluded his pursuers, taking with him all the fighting men under his control. He had sailed off in the best vessels lying at the Montreal docks, and had even taken the precaution to wreck most of the remaining boats on this part of the river. Truly, Carleton had been remarkably efficient, considering how little military strength was under his command. Montgomery could count on this wily, able opponent to cause him all kinds of trouble until he were captured, or driven from the province.

On both shores of the St. Lawrence, the French habitants and the English settlers were friendly to the Americans, as proved by the fact that for weeks on end no one had interfered with the regular journeys of the Continental army express messengers. Through them, General Montgomery was in regular communication with his roving detachments under Colonel Easton and Major Brown. Both of these officers had set up strong defense batteries on the south shore near the town of Sorel, where the St. Lawrence contracted into a relatively narrow passage. Each had increased his force of Americans with more than a hundred Canadian volunteers, and even a few Indians. It was at Sorel that Montgomery hoped to seize Carleton, or to defeat him.

The governor-general's fleet of eleven merchant vessels sped nearly fifty miles downstream from Montreal during the night of the eleventh of November and the morning of the twelfth. Just off Sorel, at noon, the wind failed. The British commander held his flotilla out of range of the American batteries for the next three days, as a contrary wind blew hard upstream, and offered no chance for escape. The Americans, meanwhile, spent the interval assembling a heavy floating battery, on which they mounted several field guns.

Then they moved out into the river to attack. Their firing, however, proved more of a nuisance than a danger. Both sides could plainly see that they were at stalemate. Carleton could not pass the Sorel headland with its heavy batteries, and the light pieces on the barge were of no serious menace.

Late in the day, under a flag of truce, Colonel Easton sent a messenger by small boat to General Carleton, arguing that with Montgomery in possession of Montreal, and American guns controlling the river at the Sorel passage, "your own situation is rendered very disagreeable." Easton then proposed that General Carleton surrender, assuring him:

"That if you will resign your fleet to me immediately, without destroying the effects on board, you and your men shall be used with due civility, together with women and children on board. To this I shall expect your direct and immediate answer. Should you neglect to do so, you will cheerfully take the consequences which will follow."

Carleton was not the type of man to give up without a fight. As he delayed sending a response to Easton's demand, the American floating battery opened fire. Carleton thereupon ordered his followers to run with the wind upstream, back toward Montreal. About twelve miles above Sorel, on the north shore, he tried to land near the village of Lavaltrie, but quickly took refuge in midstream when a scattering of Americans and French habitants opened fire on his ships. The general and his soldiers might have tried to fight their way ashore, but that would mean risking the lives of the women and children refugees from Montreal, members of officers' families, who had crowded aboard his vessels. Nor could he permit these rebels to gain possession of the several tons of powder and other military stores which he had rescued from the abandoned city. He could not stay in mid-stream forever. Yet on shore both Brown and Easton were waiting, with 32-pounders, cannon that could crush the planking of these river craft like so much paper once the gunners would get the range.

The early evening darkness of winter brought a few hours of safety to Carleton's small fleet. Early in the evening he called a council of his ranking officers and captains of the merchant ships. He may have been asking himself how long any of these civilians would remain loyal to him if they felt that escape were impossible, and resistance would bring the destruction of their vessels. He decided to abandon the idea of getting the entire group through to Quebec, and rescue what he could of the situation. In short, this meant to Carleton that he must make every effort to reach Quebec himself, in order to command its defense against the rebels. The plan that finally emerged from the council was bold and risky, but if everyone involved would do his part they would come out of this trap with far more advantage than they thought possible earlier in the day.

Captain Belette, who commanded one of the vessels equipped with at least a few guns, pledged to face the enemy gunboats on the next day and by firing and maneuvering to draw as much of their attention as possible. General Prescott and the entire force of regular soldiers were to stay with the fleet to repel boarders, and were not to surrender for three days. Before any surrender, however, Prescott was to destroy all useful arms and to dump his powder over the side.

The leading role in the drama was to be played by Captain Jean-Baptiste Bouchette, a river pilot renowned from one end of the St. Lawrence to the other for his detailed knowledge of every current, rock and snag between Quebec and Montreal. Bouchette had for years piloted his river boat up and down this difficult waterway so rapidly that his French friends had nicknamed him "La Tourtre"—the wild pigeon—after the bird of swift flight with an unerring instinct for its route home. Captain Bouchette promised Carleton that he and four oarsman would take the chance of slipping the governor past the guns of the Sorel narrows, in a whaleboat and at night. They could not wait until tomorrow night. It must be now—or perhaps never. Once past Sorel, they would stand a good chance of reaching friends downstream.

Putting himself completely into the hands of Bouchette, Carleton prepared at once for the journey. He removed his general's uniform and put on a simple suit of gray Canadian homespun, such as any villager in this country might wear. A dash of color was added by a typical red sash and red tasseled cap, while his feet were encased in a countryman's skin boots resembling Indian moccasins. There was a quick farewell, and then La Tourtre's small boat slipped away into the freezing darkness with the governor-general of Canada, traveling incognito as a fugitive in the country over which he ruled in the name of Britain's king.

Hugging close to the north shore, Bouchette steered his craft through a narrow passage between the Ile St. Ignace and the Ile du Pas, where the American patrols were least likely to see them. At one point, close to a shore battery, the rowers shipped their oars so as to make no sound, and paddled for close to an hour with their hands. Steadily the current carried the whaleboat through the danger zone toward the safety of the broad stream beyond. There was no challenge from the shore, and no firing. Unheard and unseen, the boat floated into the clear, and by daylight Carleton and his companions were close to Trois Rivières, a good-sized French town thirty miles below Sorel.

Here, as Carleton's good fortune would have it, the armed ship *Fell* commanded by Captain Napier was standing by the pier. Carleton, still in his disguise, came quietly on board, under the noses of many townsmen who were preparing to welcome the approaching American troops as their friends. Setting out at once, Captain Napier sailed the remaining eighty miles down the St. Lawrence to Quebec in two days. Early on November 19th, in a chill mist, the *Fell* passed so close to Benedict Arnold's camp a few miles above the fortress city that the American soldiers at first wondered if the ship might be carrying the vanguard of Montgomery's army, coming to their aid. All too soon, they learned that its most important passenger was their most deadly foe.

In Quebec, the arrival of General Guy Carleton set off a general rejoicing among the loyalists. For weeks now the city had been prey to rumor, doubt and fear. Lieutenant-Governor Cramahé was no military leader of stature, and was not trusted by some of Colonel MacLean's British officers. MacLean was at loggerheads with the French civilians, many of whom were not eager to take up arms against the besiegers for fear of reprisals in case the city should fall to the Americans. The French who only yesterday, it seemed, had been the victims of English conquest, could not throw away in a day the memory of a long history and embrace the British flag and military command. The scars of battle from Wolfe's bombardment of Quebec were still fresh. And many of the recent settlers from the British Isles resented the Quebec Act, because it gave undue power to the old French landlords and to the clergy. Yet, with the arrival of Governor-General Carleton, the atmosphere changed at once, for here was a leader who knew how to take command. As Thomas Ainslie, collector of customs and a captain of militia in Quebec, wrote in his diary:

"On November 19th (a happy day for Quebec!) to the unspeakable joy of the friends of the government, and to the utter dismay of the abettors of sedition and rebellion, General Carleton arrived in the armed ship *Fell,* accompanied by an armed schooner. We saw our salvation in his presence."

On the same day that Carleton reached Quebec, Colonel Easton reported to Montgomery from Sorel the surrender of General Prescott and the eleven river boats, all of which Easton sent to Montreal to transport the army to Quebec. Prescott had at least obeyed his orders to throw his powder into the river, rather than let it fall into Easton's hands. But otherwise, it seemed to both Easton and Montgomery, the British General had acted a coward's part. Under pretense of protecting the fifty women and ninety children in his ships from danger, he had surrendered the entire flotilla, and delivered a generous haul of food supplies, artillery pieces, shot, cartridges and entrenching tools.

Writing to his wife, Janet, of this new feather in his cap, Montgomery said:

> "The other day General Prescott was so obliging as to surrender himself and fourteen or fifteen land officers, with above one hundred men, besides sea officers and sailors, as prisoners of war. I blush for His Majesty's troops! Such an instance of base poltroonery I never met with! And all because we had a half-dozen cannon on the banks of the river to annoy him in his retreat.

"The Governor escaped, more's the pity! Prescott, nevertheless, is a prize. He is a cruel rascal. I have treated him with the sovereign contempt his inhumanity and barbarity merit.

"Tomorrow I hope to set out for Quebec, to join Col. Arnold, who is impatient to see us. His little army has undergone inexpressible hardships, and entered the country half-starved and half-naked. Should fortune continue her favor we may perhaps bring that business to a happy issue. In the meantime, adieu! Believe me most affectionately your

Richard Montgomery."

The American general was impatient to pursue Carleton to Quebec without losing another day in Montreal. Already the cold was severe, and ice along the river banks was becoming thicker each night. He wrote optimistically to his dear Janet, as if to allay her fears, that he was in good health and lived "in hopes to see you in six weeks." But in his written reports to General Schuyler and in his private correspondence addressed to Robert Livingston, Montgomery was careful not to arouse false hopes of easy success.

"I am ashamed of dating my letter from hence," he wrote Schuyler, after he had been in Montreal a full twelve days, "but day after day I have been delayed, without a possibility of getting to Arnold's assistance. Tomorrow, I believe, I shall sail with two or three hundred men, some mortars and other artillery."

He had no more than eight hundred fit men, Montgomery wrote, but he could easily enlist as many Canadian volunteers as he could equip and feed, "while affairs wear so promising a prospect." For the moment, his main worries concerned matters other than figthing—the need to send "more hard money here immediately, as paper will not yet go down"; the fact that the engineer officer repairing the St. John's barracks as a winter garrison had quit his post; the friction between his troops and the Tories in Montreal, who still walked the streets freely carrying arms; and the bad debts left behind by several Continental army comissaries. Again, as so many times before, the young general pleaded with Schuyler to send a committee of the Continental Congress to Canada, one with the ability and authority to take charge of civil affairs:

"I really have not weight enough to carry on business by myself."

On the eve of embarking for the trip to join Arnold before Quebec, Montgomery wrote in the utmost confidence to his brother-in-law Robert what difficulties lay ahead, as he saw them. There would be no more easy surrenders; a grim winter of fighting and death confronted the Continental army in Canada, and the Congress should face the facts.

"For the good fortune which has hitherto attended us, I am, I hope, sufficiently thankful," Montgomery wrote. "But this very fortune, good as it has been, will become a serious and insurmountable evil, should it lead Congress either to overrate our means, or to underrate the difficulties we have yet to contend with.

"I need not tell you that, till Quebec is taken, Canada is unconquered. And that, to accomplish this, we must resort to siege, investment, or storm."

Montgomery explained that a siege, requiring digging entrenchments and battering the city with artillery, was "out of the question." The ground at Quebec would be frozen too hard, and the Americans did not have artillery equal to the task of reducing Quebec's stout walls. Investment, which meant surrounding the city and starving it into surrender by cutting off its connections with the nearby farm country, would require far more than the eight hundred combat men now with him and Arnold's force.

So it comes down to taking Quebec by storm, Montgomery wrote Robert. The advantage would be with the attackers, who could pick their time and place against a force of weary defenders, fatigued from being forced to maintain constant alerts, night and day. One hope might lie in Carleton's becoming desperate, and coming forth from the protection of the ramparts to fight in the open. If so, it would be a boon, for Carleton would be committing the same error of which Montcalm was guilty in 1759.

"In this last idea there is a glimmering of hope. Wolfe's success was a lucky hit, or rather a series of such hits. All sober and scientific calculation was aginst him until Montcalm, permitting his courage to get the better of his discretion, gave up the advantages of his fortress and came out to try his strength on the plain.

"Carleton, who was Wolfe's quartermaster-general, understands this well, and, it is to be feared, will not follow the Frenchman's example."

The coming battle of Quebec was surrounded by uncertainties, Montgomery concluded, but of one thing Congress could be sure: if it were not won by the middle of April, "the game will be up." For with the breaking of the ice-jam in the St. Lawrence, the British fleet would be able to resupply and reinforce the garrison "in spite of anything we can do to prevent it." Then, Montgomery wrote, he would be helpless, "because the troops are not engaged beyond that term, and will not be prevailed upon to stay a day longer."

As Montgomery's fleet of river ships left the piers of Montreal on November 28th and caught the wind and current for Quebec, the Continental brigadier of five months' standing realized that the next few weeks, perhaps the coming few days, would bring his business in Canada to a climax. Now there was no turning back, either for General Guy Carleton or for Richard Montgomery. The fox had escaped him, but was now cornered in his lair. He, Montgomery, was the hunter, ironically in the same position that General James Wolfe had been sixteen years ago.

What changes had come over the world, and into his own life, during those years! In that far-off time when he had worn the bright red British uniform with pride, he had cheered with his comrades when the news came that their flag now flew over the fortress of Quebec. Yet now, through the inscrutable ways that God manipulates the affairs of men, he was about to attack that fortress, that uniform and that very flag. For as long as Carleton held that one vital square mile of Canadian soil, one of the vast million miles in the province, American liberty would not be secure.

❦ 7 ❧

Duel for Quebec

O F all cities in North America, Quebec, by a blend of its geographical position and the military engineering lavished upon it, had the strongest defenses. Indeed, it was the very advantage offered by the nature of the terrain that led to its development, during the century and a half of French rule, as the primary port and fortress of New France.

The major part of Quebec City stood on the northeast tip of a long finger-shaped plateau extending above the left bank of the St. Lawrence River, just upstream from the point where it broadened out into a slow-moving tidal estuary leading to the Atlantic. From this height the city commanded a view across the river to a similar tableland on the southeast shore. The distance between them, a scant one thousand yards, could be commanded easily by cannon, and small boats in skilled hands could make the crossing in a matter of minutes. Thus, the guns of the city could always have the advantage of height over any attack by ships on the St. Lawrence. In the years since the English conquest of the province, the walls were strengthened and their armament increased by the emplacement of heavy 32-pounders.

Nearly three-fourths of the perimeter of the fortified city was protected by a rocky cliff so steep in most places as to defy scaling, even under the most favorable conditions. A thick wall surmounted this natural palisade on three sides of the town, following its edge in the shape of a rough-drawn letter "C" around nearly one and a half miles in its curved length. Poking through gun embrasures in the walls on all sides were cannon placed so as to command the ground and river in every direction outside the fortifications. The broad gap between the points of the wall-capped precipice lay directly across the open tableland west and somewhat south of the main part of Quebec. Across this sector extending nearly two-thirds of a mile, the fortification ring was closed by an immense wall of heavy masonry, protected by six jutting bastions that offered the chance for the defenders to bring flanking fire against their attackers.

By any calculation, the western flank of the city was the one most favorable for the assembly of an enemy force, given the virtual impossibility of anyone's climbing the cliffs on the other three sides. Here, in fact, General Wolfe had drawn up in battle array in September 1759; and following in his trail, Benedict Arnold had approached the city from this side in mid-November. Generally open meadowland, dotted with only a few scattered trees and bushes, this terrain rose gently along the two roads leading through the two city gates opening on this side, until, from a point about a half mile from the walls, one could actually look slightly down into the town. This was the area called variously the Heights of Abraham or the Plains of Abraham, after an early settler named Abraham Martin who had grazed his flocks on the rolling meadows here.

Farming was productive in the country around Quebec, as it was throughout the St. Lawrence Valley. Consequently, since the English had become masters of the province, any number of gentlemen had settled, bought land, built fine houses and prospered with the growth of the population and economic life of Quebec. It was the more affluent tradesmen, landowners and servants of the crown, both English and some of French origin, who lived in the Upper Town of Quebec, that part surrounded by the connecting fortifications and cliffs.

But there was another part of Quebec, known as the Lower Town, built upon the narrow strip of low-lying land hemmed in between the overhanging cliffs and the river's edge. Where the cliff curved sharply around to the north and west, a sluggish, winding tributary of the St. Lawrence, the St. Charles River, offered a shallow harbor for smaller craft. The waterfront of the Lower Town of Quebec was therefore partly on the larger river, and extended around the tip of the promontory toward the mouth of the St. Charles. In this section of Quebec were the commerical houses and warehouses, and here the dwellings of the poor class of people were huddled tightly together in streets so narrow that the sunlight rarely penetrated into them.

One could reach the Lower Town from either end on foot by scrambling along a narrow path between the rocky cliff and the shoreline. But heavy loads could enter or leave it only by ship, or by the one street leading to it from the Upper City. This was a serpentine road blasted from the palisade long before, one that taxed the strongest horses to their utmost. Appropriately, it was called Rue de la Montagne, or in English, Mountain Road. In preparing this entry to the Upper Town for defense, the French and the British following them had built massive parapets, from which a hundred riflemen and twenty guns could fire down from protected positions on any party of enemies so bold as to try to force their way up this slope.

Such, in general, was the physical situation in which Governor-General Guy Carleton found himself at the end of November 1775. Carleton expected Benedict Arnold to reappear at any time on the Heights of Abraham to the west, and Montgomery was coming down the St. Lawrence to his aid. During Carleton's absence from the city, the superintendent of military works, James Thompson, had been working vigorously to strengthen the defenses of Quebec. He had stripped the boat yards of all available spar-timber, and cutting them to length had erected double wooden barriers at both ends of the Lower Town. He had also built stout picket fences with loopholes for firing, on the high ground outside the west walls of the Upper Town, as a front line of defense against assault.

Carleton's main concern, therefore, was not with the state of his fortifications or munitions. He was well equipped with powder, shot, cannon and the standard military food-stores on which the British soldier was accustomed to live through the winter. The governor was extremely doubtful, however, about the men on whom he must rely to hold the city—both those under arms and the civilian population behind them. In Montreal he had found the populace completely unwilling to join him and his small command of regulars to defend the town. He had been further dismayed by reports coming from all parts of the St. Lawrence Valley that the Canadians were largely in sympathy with the American rebels, were supplying them with food, housing them and assisting them with information on the movements of British troops. Even here in Quebec, he was informed, some men who had joined the defense militia early in the fall had lately refused to bear arms and stand watch at the city walls. From one end of the town to the other, both English and French habitants were questioning whether they should bring down on Quebec another bombardment like that in the days of Montcalm and Wolfe.

Quickly seizing the initiative, Carleton summoned a council of the ranking men in Quebec, including Lieutenant-Governor Cramahé, Colonel MacLean, captains of the ships now in port and a few gentlemen who had been active in rallying a citizens' militia. Every disloyal person, Carleton told them, must be expelled from the city at once, because he meant to fight to the end. He would not risk being stabbed in the back by rebel sympathizers.

On November 22nd the governor issued a sweeping proclamation, the purpose of which was "to rid the town of all useless, disloyal and treacherous persons" who would not serve in the militia. These people were ordered "to quit the town in four days from the date hereof, together with their wives and children, and to withdraw themselves out of the limits of the District of Quebec before the first day of December next, under pain of being treated as rebels or spies, if, thereafter, they shall be found within the said limits."

Carleton's order led a good many English families in sympathy with the Americans to pack their belongings and take to the wintry roads, in order to find shelter in villages far enough from Quebec for safety. When the purge was completed, the muster roll of militia in Quebec totaled about eight hundred and sixty men, with more French names on it than before, but a serious decline among the English. How much genuine heart for fighting there was among these remaining militiamen was a secret that they alone knew, since their service was compelled by a strong-willed governor-general with an array of armed power at his disposal. Above the citizens under arms he had only a few regulars—twenty-two Royal Artillerymen, seventy Royal Fusiliers and thirty-five Royal Marines. But Colonel MacLean had under him two hundred and thirty members of his corps of emigrants, mainly veterans of the previous war. There were four hundred British and French-Canadian seamen under fifty ships' officers. One hundred twenty skilled military artificers, such as gunsmiths, powder-makers and carpenters, filled out Carleton's roster of eighteen hundred men engaged to defend the town. All told, the walls of Quebec encompassed some five thousand men, women and children after the gates closed behind those whom the governor-general had expelled.

One day's march upstream from Quebec, at Point aux Trembles, Richard Montgomery at last joined forces with Benedict Arnold, almost three full months after entering the province of Quebec. Despite the ragged appearance of their clothing, Arnold's men impressed Montgomery with the ruggedness of their physique and their morale. These men and their leader had been put to the most severe hardship in their wilderness march. Having passed through the cruel test of survival of the fittest, the troops before him represented the best in Arnold's original force of one thousand. The weak and the cowardly had largely been eliminated—something that Montgomery could not say of his own corps.

On December 2nd, as he prepared to march for the Plains of Abraham to confront General Carleton, Montgomery had a force totaling just over eight hundred men. Of these five hundred had been with Arnold, and only three hundred had ˋ descended the St. Lawrence River Valley with him. Others were strung out in patrols and garrisons along the supply line reaching back to Ticonderoga. It was essential that he receive reinforcements from the direction of Montreal. But the crust of ice extending farther out from the river banks after every freezing night showed that the end of navigation for this season would be reached within a few days.

By December 5th, the Americans had moved into position before and around the fortress city. One small detachment with a couple of light field guns was stationed on the heights across the river at Levis. The downriver edge of the city was left completely open, there being no means of attacking Quebec from there, nor any danger of escape over the ice, which was still too thin for traffic. To the north and northwest, outside the walls of the city, Arnold's forces occupied houses and barns in three small suburbs. These were named Le Palais, a cluster of dwellings near the old French governor's palace and the Palace Gate; St. Roch, which extended several hundred yards to the northwest; and St. Jean,* which lay near the St. Jean gate, just north of the road leading from Quebec west toward St. Foy.

At the order of General Carleton, the armed defenders had driven a number of families from the houses that lay closest to the city walls, and burned the buildings down, in order to deprive the attackers of shelter. But most Quebec houses were designed in the old French peasant tradition, and built with solid stone walls more than a foot thick, to

* French form of St. John's.

withstand the severe winters of this latitude. They were therefore not entirely leveled, either by the torch or by cannon-
balls fired at them from very close range. Nor could the governor smash down all the houses that would endanger his
defenses from this quarter without giving the owners cause
to revolt. So, at best, his scorched-earth program was carried
out in only a few places, and the Americans camped under
adequate cover within two hundred to five hundred yards
of the Quebec ramparts.

Montgomery's force spread out thinly along the Plains of
Abraham, west of the city. Soldiers occupied every available
house that could shelter them from the winds that continu-
ally swept this height of land, cutting through their ragged
clothing and freezing exposed hands, feet and faces with the
pain of a thousand needles. Patrols dug shelter points as
best they could through the snow and frozen ground near
the brow of the plateau, in order to keep the city under close
observation. And for the first few days Montgomery's main
concern was to insure that each officer stressed to his ser-
geants and men the importance of guard duty. During his
tour on post, each man was to stay alert, keep his powder
dry and be ready to sound the alarm in case of any commo-
tion from the direction of the city. Meanwhile, the rest of
the men were organizing cooking and sleeping quarters,
bringing forward the artillery and mortars, and preparing
gun emplacements from which to fire them.

Montgomery selected Holland House, two miles from
Quebec on the St. Foy road, as his headquarters. It was a
stately house, owned by Major Samuel Holland, who was
known throughout Quebec and the New England colonies
as the foremost surveyor and map-maker in the service of
the crown in America. When hostilities broke out earlier in

the year, Holland, then in Massachusetts, had been approached by representatives of General Washington to sound his views on assisting in the campaign of resistance. But Holland had stayed staunchly by the king, the British army and what he considered his duty. As Montgomery took over his house in Quebec, Major Holland was being held in New Jersey under arrest as a Tory too dangerous to permit at large.

In a lengthy report written to General Schuyler from Holland House on December 5th, Montgomery showed himself in an optimistic mood. "Nothing shall be wanting on my part to reap the advantage of our good fortune," he wrote. "Mr. Carleton, who is I suppose ashamed to show himself in England, is now in town, and puts on a show of defense. The works of Quebec are extremely extensive, and very incapable of being defended." He went on to emphasize in somewhat scornful terms the poor quality and small size of the defense garrison, and the fact that most of the citizens under arms would not stand "the fatigues of a siege, and wish to see matters accommodated amicably."

Montgomery then outlined his strategy of diverting his opponent in front, then striking his rear:

"I propose amusing Mr. Carleton with a formal attack, erecting batteries, etc., but mean to assault the works, I believe, towards the lower town, which is the weakest part.

"I have this day written to Mr. Carleton, and also to the inhabitants, which I hope will have some effect. I shall be very sorry to be reduced to this mode of attack, because I know the melancholy consequences, but the approaching severe season and the weakness of the garrison, together with the nature of the works, point it out too strongly to be passed by."

Then, apparently dwelling in his mind on the mutilation and death—the "melancholy consequences"—that an armed assault on Quebec would bring to both sides, Montgomery tempered his earlier optimism with an element of doubt:

"Fortune often baffles the sanguine expectations of poor mortals. I am not intoxicated with the favors I have received at her hands, but I do think there is a fair prospect of success."

The report to General Schuyler was highly enthusiastic over Arnold and his men: "I find Colonel Arnold's corps an exceeding fine one, inured to fatigue and well accustomed to cannon shot (at Cambridge). There is a style of discipline among them much superior to what I have been used to see in this campaign. He himself is active, intelligent and enterprising . . . Indeed I must say he has brought with him many pretty young men."

Supplies and men. These were the two themes to which Montgomery repeatedly returned in appealing to Schuyler for continued support. He had been forced by necessity at Montreal to offer the clothing and the dollar bounty in order to induce the men to follow him to Quebec. He hoped that Schuyler would get the approval of Congress for this decision in the field. And when Easton's detachment had seized General Prescott's vessels on the river, the cold weather and their half-naked condition forced him to let them help themselves from the public stores aboard. The greater part of the clothing was, of course, fair prize of war subject to seizure; but Montgomery insisted to Schuyler that some of it, "such as immediately belonged to the prisoners, must be paid for, as it was their own property. We shall have more time hereafter to settle this affair."

Governor Carleton's purge of the city, Montgomery reported, had turned out well for the Continental army: "The Governor has been so kind as to send out of town many of our friends who refused to do military duty; among them several very intelligent men, capable of doing me considerable service. One of them, a Mr. Antill, I have appointed chief engineer, Mr. Mott and his suite having returned home."

Should Quebec be taken, Montgomery wrote, and the hostilities with Great Britain continue, ten thousand men would be needed to secure the province against reconquest by the British. "The Canadians will be our friends as long as we are able to maintain our ground, but they must not be depended upon, especially for defensive operations.... I don't know whether I informed you, that it was in vain to think of engaging the troops for twelve months. The 15th of April, which allows them time to plant their corn upon returning home, was all I dared to ask. I hope the proper measures will be taken for sending fresh troops into the country before that time."

On the same day, in a short letter to his Janet, Montgomery made light of the winter and the difficulties facing him. She was surely not writing to him as often as he was writing to her, he teased. Yes, he would remember to bring her a beaver blanket from Quebec "if I get safe out of this affair," and marten skins for Janet's mother. And Mrs. Livingston could rest easily on the safety of her young son Harry, who was under his care. He was safe and causing no trouble, though he was a bit imprudent. As for the coming attack on Quebec, he made light of it:

"They are a good deal alarmed in town, and with some reason. The garrison is little to be depended upon, and very weak in proportion to the extent of the works. I wish it were well over with all my heart, and sigh for home like a New England . . . May I have the pleasure of seeing you there soon! Till then, adieu!"

The general's light tone belied the facts. There had been more than a foot of snow on the ground when he had joined Arnold, and the next three days had seen rain turning to sleet, then a hard overnight freeze, then more drifting snow carried by sharp winds that shifted from northeast around to the west. This was the most severe weather that any of these men from more temperate climes had known in their lives, and their main preoccupation was keeping warm. Day and night, sentinels were repeatedly caught shirking their duty, huddling in a sheltered spot in the lee of a barn or house, out of the wind and snow, where they could warm themselves by a fire, stamp their feet and beat their hands to restore circulation. Time after time they had to be reprimanded, but repeated their offenses, to Montgomery's despair. On December 6th, in his general orders issued from Holland House, Montgomery pleaded with his officers to show the minimal degree of discipline that the situation demanded.

"The general recommends to the officers of the different guards that they be more vigilant in visiting their out sentinels and teach them their duty, to wit—they ought by no means to suffer any persons to pass them at night without ordering to stand until the guard is turned out to inquire the counter sign from such persons and then to let them pass."

On the very next day Montgomery felt impelled to repeat in his general orders that he expected "the officers of the guard to observe the orders with respect to the vigilance of the guard, that no surprise by their neglect may happen."

And again on December 8th the commander called his officers' attention to the need for military discipline, ". . . so much the more when we are in sight of the enemy. It is therefore the general orders that the officers commanding regiments as well as those commanding companies with their subalterns must be extremely careful that former orders are put into strict execution, as also the soldiers to be repeatedly examined whether their arms and ammunition are in good order, as the general expects the officers to be answerable for the neglect of these orders if found disobeyed by the soldiers."

While Montgomery was struggling as diplomatically as he could to obtain the cooperation of his officers, Arnold's force close to the northwest ramparts were actively engaging in a soldier's sport—sharpshooting. Sneaking as close to the city walls as they dared, and taking cover behind stone walls and in the upper rooms of houses in the Palais and St. Roch suburbs, several of the best riflemen kept up a sniping fire at any exposed figure on the walls of Quebec. It was easy to see a sentry clearly outlined against the sky. Hardly a day passed without one of the defenders being wounded, or killed outright. Yet retaliatory fire from the ramparts was largely wasted, because Arnold's men were so well hidden, or because they ducked under cover after firing a shot.

During the second week in December, night working parties on the heights hacked away at the frozen ground to a sufficient depth to loosen the soil, and prepared positions for the mortars and light artillery pieces that Montgomery had brought with him from Montreal. The main battery was on the Heights of Abraham, about a half mile due west of the St. Louis gate. Montgomery had to place it that close, both to act as a diversion that General Carleton's forces could see, and because his light guns, mostly ranging from 2-pounders to 9-pounders, could not fire with much effect from a greater distance.

To protect their batteries, the usual method of artillery-men was to surround the guns with vertical fascines, which were long cylindrical baskets woven of pliable twigs, into which heavy rocks and earth were tamped. But to speed matters, in view of the difficulty of digging in this frozen climate, the Americans filled their fascines with packed snow, then threw water over them so as to freeze them into solid pillars of ice. It was a clever and original experiment, "typical of Yankee ingenuity"—as one of Montgomery's officers described it in his journal. But ice proved no substitute for mixed earth and rock. A few well-directed cannon shot from the ramparts of Quebec severely damaged the improvised gun emplacements within the next several days. Montgomery's heaviest gun was a 12-pounder. Carleton, on the other hand, had scores of 18-, 24- and 32-pound cannon. Montgomery was completely outgunned.

The men in Arnold's sector had better luck, however. By December 10th they had opened a battery of mortars from a position in St. Roch that it was difficult for the British gunners to strike. Not only was the mortar emplacement well disguised among the jumble of gray stone walls and roofs in the suburb, but the defense gunners who were in a position to fire on St. Roch were exposed to attack by Arnold's snipers. So for several days and nights, as this cat-and-mouse game continued, the American mortar batteries lobbed solid iron ball shot almost at random into the town, smashing into roofs indiscriminately without doing serious damage to the city's defenses. Nor did they profit from the fright of a few inhabitants of the town when they threw in hollow shells, fused on firing and timed to explode after thudding into a Quebec house or street. They were not aiming at targets of military importance, just the town in general.

Still the wind blew, and the snows came down, drifting thick around every projecting rock and wall. In the American camp it became steadily more difficult to move easily from one house to another. Sentries stuck close to the paths they had marked out in making their rounds from company headquarters, to squad barrack-houses and observation posts, and to the batteries. Within the city, a hurricane from the northwest on December 11th covered every house and street with a sheet of ice, so that there was almost no stirring about without putting on "creepers," the spiked overshoe which the French Canadian had long been accustomed to wearing at such times.

Both sides felt their own suffering from the severe weather, and uncertainty added to their discomfort. Both leaders were apprehensive lest the enemy enjoyed advantages that were hidden from his eyes. At the same time, both Carleton and Montgomery were well aware of the weaknesses in their own camps. Carleton could never tell for certain what the citizens were thinking behind his back, despite his air of firm confidence that "these rebels" would freeze or starve outside the walls of Quebec. Montgomery, for his part, could not be sure that his men, or even his officers, would attack the armed town with real courage when the time was ripe.

Neither commander was able to control the flow of intelligence that filtered steadily in both directions between the besieged and the besieging force. Every few nights a deserter from the Quebec militia, or simply a civilian refugee, would sneak from a small, narrow gate near Le Palais, or would somehow get over the wall, to bring news of the garrison's numbers, the state of public morale, or the fact that the American artillery had done little damage in the town. An occasional deserter or a civilian from outside would carry word to the fortress of the disposition of Montgomery's forces, the illness among his men, and his lack of heavy artillery. Thus, each commander knew fairly closely the strength and weakness of the other.

As the tense, cold days and nights passed with each side staying watchfully in position, and trading only occasional rifle and cannon shots, the two commanders began to play at psychological warfare. Isolated cases of smallpox both within Quebec and in its suburbs were magnified by British and Americans alike into reports of a raging epidemic in the other's camp. Carleton's officers helped to circulate the rumor among the civilians that General Montgomery was the same man who, as a British officer under Wolfe, had become notorious throughout this countryside for having ordered cruel burning of peasant homes and summary execution of French habitants. Although he was a totally different person, it was said that the bestial "Captain Montgomery" of the previous war had returned to repeat his inhuman crimes. This time he had promised his men an orgy of looting within the town, and should he enter its gates, no one and no property would be safe. The Continentals had plundered ever since they entered the province of Quebec, Carleton's rumors said, and the merchants of Montreal had been forced to buy their safety at a price of £16,000 sterling.

Another story that spread within the city was to the effect

that a cannonball from Quebec had smashed Montgomery's carriage and killed its horse, just a few seconds after he had stepped from it. Still another, apparently designed to show the leader of the invading rebels as a profane man, held that Montgomery had "sworn he would eat his Christmas dinner in Quebec, or in Hell!"

The morning of December 15th dawned mild and clear, with a gentle easterly wind. At nine o'clock Montgomery sent Captain John MacPherson, his trusted aide-de-camp, forward to the west wall of the city, accompanied by a drummer and bearing a flag of truce. The defenders grounded their arms as an officer called out to MacPherson to state his business.

"A message from General Montgomery to Governor Carleton!" MacPherson shouted. There was considerable calling back and forth as word was carried to Carleton at his headquarters that the rebel officer had brought a demand for surrender. Back came the brusque reply: the governor would not admit a messenger, nor would he treat with *Mister* Montgomery by any channel! MacPherson was told to make his way off from the walls, if he knew what was good for him. Angered, MacPherson shouted back that Governor Carleton would "remember this." As he slogged off through the snow with his drummer and white flag, the British officer on the wall had difficulty restraining his soldiers from shooting at the retreating figures.

Montgomery had other ways of reaching Carleton, however. Already he had employed a woman messenger, who wanted to join her family in the town when the troops pushed her from her house in St. Roch. The woman was admitted to the Palais gate at night, and gave to the guards Montgomery's letter addressed to the governor. Carleton made a show of not reading it, in order to display his contempt for the enemies of the crown. He had the woman brought into his headquarters, so that she could witness his throwing Montgomery's message into the fire, stating that it had not even been read. Afterward the woman was pushed from the gate, and told to carry back word to the Americans of what General Carleton had done.

Montgomery had offered Carleton a safe conduct back to England if he would surrender the town. Perhaps the younger man had a faint hope that his proud opponent might accept, even though he must have realized that Carleton was not such a weakling as to save his skin without honor. But now that the British commander had insulted him again by not even accepting his aide-de-camp under a flag of truce, and by persisting in not calling him by his military rank, Montgomery lost patience. This time he caused several copies of a new letter to be written, had them attached to arrows and shot over the walls on December 16th by daylight. In that way they would certainly be seen by several people, and their contents become generally known. This letter Carleton was unable to suppress.

In it, Montgomery complained of "the personal ill-treatment I have received at your hands" and "the cruelty you have shown to the unhappy prisoners you have taken." He pointed out "the absurdity of resistance," in view of the fact that Carleton's garrison was largely made up of friends of the United Colonies "who wish to see us within the walls," and "a few of the worst troops who call themselves soldiers." No help could reach Carleton, and he was cut off from supplies, Montgomery continued. On the other hand, the letter went on:

"I am at the head of troops accustomed to success, confident of the righteousness of the cause they are engaged in, inured to danger and fatigue, and so highly incensed at your inhumanity, illiberal abuse, and the ungenerous means employed to prejudice them in the minds of the Canadians, that it is with difficulty I restrain them, till my batteries are ready, from assaulting your works, which would afford them a fair opportunity of ample vengeance and just retaliation . . .

"Should you persist in an unwarrantable defense, the consequence be upon your own head. Beware of destroying stores of any sort, as you did at Montreal or in the river. If you do, by Heavens there will be no mercy shown!"

There was a large element of bluff in Montgomery's message, for he was by no means ready to launch his assault. Reinforcements, which he had been anxiously awaiting for two weeks since joining Arnold, had still not arrived, so he realized he was still outnumbered by nearly two to one. Dangerous as it might be for the Continentals, however, a sortie from the walls led by the British regulars might give him the luck he needed to turn the present stalemate into a victorious seizure of the town. For if Carleton should send out even two or three hundred of his most reliable men to attack Arnold's troops in the northwest suburbs, the civilians of Quebec might take possession of the town in their absence.

But Carleton had never felt sure of his militiamen, of either nationality, and for that reason had interspersed British regulars among both French and English armed civilians in every guard unit. The governor had no intention of coming out into the deep snows of the plain or the suburbs, when time was on his side. His walls were rugged enough to stand anything Montgomery's batteries could throw at them. His tactic was to hold tight and stay alert.

With Carleton's flat refusal to consider surrender, Montgomery knew that he must plan to attack just as soon as more men would join him from Montreal. Every day, and every night, he lost more men to frostbite and fevers. Deserters were drifting away into the snowbound countryside. Already the number disabled by illness greatly exceeded the dozen or so killed by British fire. The longer this army should remain encamped before Quebec, the weaker it would become.

The word was passed to the officers that the men were to be prepared for an imminent attack. And to sharpen their willingness to take the necessary risks Montgomery felt compelled, against his every instinct as a gentleman and officer, to announce to the troops that they might share in all military loot to be taken "as soon as the city is in our hands and the inhabitants disarmed." The general, he declared, "is confident a vigorous and spirited attack must be attended with success. The troops shall have the effects of the governor's garrison and of such as have been active in misleading the inhabitants and distressing the friends of liberty equally divided among them."

The defenders were understandably nervous, anticipating one night after another the attack they felt sure was coming. At four o'clock in the morning on the sixteenth, less than a day after MacPherson's futile parley at the wall, a sentry by the Palais gate shouted that "six hundred men" were advancing from the nearby suburb. At once the drummers beat the to arms signal, and the great bell in Quebec cathedral sounded the alarm. Every man in Quebec hasted to his post, arms in hand. But no enemy appeared. All was still outside the fortification. When daylight finally came, all that could be seen from the walls through the driving snow was a peaceful countryside buried in a blanket of white, through which poked a jagged rock, the dark form of a stone house, or a lone, leafless tree. Not a shot was fired for nearly three days of storm and cold, as Montgomery anxiously awaited reinforcements.

During the long storm, the American general in a pensive mood wrote letters in anticipation of the impending test, to his father-in-law, to Robert, and to his wife Janet. Although his soul must have been deeply troubled by the inevitable fatal consequences of storming the city—death to an untold number of men on both sides—he tried to maintain a broader view of the undertaking. If we take Quebec, he wrote to Judge Livingston, the province can be defended against a British attempt to recover it. But it is essential that the Continental army be masters of the city, for otherwise the Canadians will not send representatives to Congress. Then, turning to personal matters, he urged the Judge to help secure the services of General Charles Lee, proposing him as "the properest person to command here."

"Should my good fortune give me success I shall as soon as possible return home. I have lost the ambition which once sweetened a military life. A sense of duty is my only spring of action. I must leave the field to those who have a more powerful incentive . . . Should the scene change, I shall always be ready to contribute my mite to the public safety."

The following day, in a letter to the younger Robert Livingston, Montgomery detailed his reasons for wanting a committee of the Continental Congress sent to the province of Quebec. He had been forced, he wrote, "to act out of my own head," as in his summary decision to clothe the troops with captured British uniforms. "A committee would have seen my distress," he continued, "the danger I ran of being totally forsaken by the troops and the difficulty I had, even high as I bid, to prevail on a few to go with me to Mr. Arnold's assistance, where a prize of such value was at stake."

Shifting to the coming attack, Montgomery's letter breathed optimism, perhaps more than he really felt was justified: "The troops seem willing for an escalade, the only mode of attack that can succeed at this season, and considering our lack of artillery. I have had a diversionary battery almost destroyed, they using 32-pounders to our 6- and 12-pounders.

"I think the works two miles in extent, some parts very weak. I'll make two attacks in the night. I think I have a great chance of succeeding. At any rate, it is worth the experiment. AUDACES FORTUNA JUVAT * is almost an axiom!"

Almost as if communicating with Robert were the deepest of personal pleasures which he was loath to bring to an end, Montgomery wrote on, discussing ways to fortify the Hudson at West Point, suggesting revival of the medieval catapult for defense of the river, inquiring into possible approaches by Congress to an ally in Europe, and asking how long Congress would keep up its attempts for accommodation with Great Britain. The thought of a final break with the mother country, Montgomery revealed, was something he could not yet accept, even now: "I hope and do verily believe the Ministry will not reduce us to this melancholy necessity."

* Fortune favors the bold.

Most of all, the general before Quebec longed for peace, and the chance to exchange ideas like civilized men with his dearest and closest friend, whose intellect he admired: "When, my dear Robert, shall we meet in peace and quietness and ride our favorite hobby horse? ORAS QUANDO EGO TE ASPICIAM! * Adieu, my dear Robert. May your happy talents be ever directed to the good of mankind!"

To Janet, as he had before through long weeks of the Canadian campaign, Montgomery wrote in a gay, bantering tone, as if to make light of his difficulties by not even mentioning them. He did not touch on the bitterness of the Quebec winter, nor the strength of his adversary, nor the coming attack, with all its risks. He dwelt instead on his pleasure at hearing from Janet, and how much he wanted to spend the rest of his life at her side without seeking adventures or military glory again:

"I wish most sincerely to sit by my own fireside. Let others by their military talents seek for applause. Give me an inglorious country life. I hope the public affairs will never have occasion again for my service."

He teased her gently for having asked him to send her longer letters: "But are you not unreasonable to expect long letters in a style as if I had nothing of greater importance upon my mind than the chit-chat of friends? All you asked of me at setting out was frequent short letters to acquaint you of my health. Now you have changed your demands. You see what unreasonable creatures you women are, and how hard to be satisfied."

The weather, and the delay in the arrival of reinforcements, gave Montgomery the time to pen his letters from Holland House. A bitterly cold east wind brought snow on

---

* Say when shall I look upon you again!

the seventeenth, and again on the eighteenth, and still again on the nineteenth. Desultory firing between St. Roch and St. Jean and the sentries on the walls was interrupted by an occasional angry explosion from one of the big guns, fired as if in desperation in the general direction of the deadly Continental sharpshooters. A tour of sentry duty was sheer misery on the ramparts, where the wind blasted at its most ferocious strength, freezing a man's musket so he could scarcely bear to touch its metal parts. But the continual deepening of the snow brought a measure of comfort to Carleton and his forces, because it meant that the attackers would have great difficulty plowing through the drifts carrying their heavy scaling ladders. And at either end of the Lower Town, where the hastily built wooden barriers formed the weakest part of Quebec's defense perimeter, the accumulating snow and ice would impede the attackers.

At ten o'clock on the night of December 22nd, two figures were seen stumbling through the darkness toward the Lower Town barrier at a cluster of houses called Près de Ville, which was nestled in the narrow space between the rocky cliff and the jumbled ice of the St. Lawrence banks. Admitted to the town after identifying themselves as friends, the men turned out to be a deserter from the Continentals and an escaped prisoner, bringing vital information. The former prisoner was Joshua Wolf, a civilian, who was clerk for Colonel Henry Caldwell, a wealthy British landowner now with General Carleton. Caldwell's mansion, not far from Holland House, was occupied by the Americans. For the past three weeks, Wolf had been allowed to perform some of his regular duties as supervisor of the Caldwell estate, while being kept under surveillance. But with the aid of a bottle of rum, judiciously poured for his thirsty guard, Wolf had manged to escape, and slipping unnoticed down to the river bank he had made his way to the Près de Ville barrier, bringing a deserter with him.

Montgomery, Wolf reported, was planning to attack on the first dark night. As far as he could tell, the general had received the reinforcements he required, and the Americans had stocked hundreds of scaling ladders. A great many Canadians were with them, Wolf said, and every man was promised £200 worth of plunder when the city would be in their hands.

As a result of the information brought by Joshua Wolf, Carleton ordered one thousand men to be in readiness on the night of the twenty-third to repulse an attack. The governor-general himself slept in his clothes at the Franciscan priory, which he had adopted as his command post because of its key position in the Upper Town. The night passed quietly, until the early hours, when another deserter staggered through the heavy snow to the St. Jean gate, fired his musket in the air and clamored to be let in. The heavy gate being fastened shut by barricades of ice, the man was hauled up to the ramparts with ropes. The attack, the new informant declared, had been put off because of Wolf's escape. But unless his own desertion should cause another postponement, it was coming the next night.

Meanwhile, Montgomery and his officers were having the most extreme difficulties in getting their troops ready. Every day the miserably cold men were straggling about from one shelter or fire to another, letting their firearms become caked with ice, permitting their cartridges to be soaked and rendered useless. Daily the general had to repeat his orders that officers were to be responsible for the condition of their men's arms, and their readiness to fall in when the call to attack should come.

Montgomery's delay in ordering the final thrust against Quebec was due not just to the severity of the weather and the absence of a dark night to mask his approach. Dissension had broken out in Arnold's force. Three company commanders had told the general they would positively not take part in the attack under Arnold's leadership. There had been hot words among them, and Arnold was not a man to hold his temper when angered. But the fact that most of his men had engaged to serve only through the end of the year made them most hesitant to risk their lives in the final week of military duty. Why, many of the volunteers must have asked themselves, should they risk being shot down like dogs in the snow at the end of December, when on New Year's Day they would be free to go home?

Perhaps half of Montgomery's total force before Quebec were in this state of mind. The rest were either men who were determined to stay throughout, whatever might come, or who had signed to serve until April of the next year. But without the backbone of Arnold's corps putting their hearts into storming the city, Montgomery could see his hopes of victory dwindling to nothing within another week or ten days. Calling each of the disaffected officers into conference, he implored them to stand by him and do their patriotic duty, while they yet had time. Reporting the incident secretly to General Schuyler on the day after Christmas, Montgomery wrote:

"The three discontented companies are within a few days of being free from their engagements. I must try every means to prevent their departure, and in this matter I am much embarrassed. Their officers have offered to stay, provided they may join some other corps. This is resentment against Arnold, and will hurt him so much that I do not think I can consent to it."

The dissension had now gone too deep for repair. Montgomery knew that he must rally his army at once for the attack, or his chance would be gone. On the twenty-seventh he sent the alert message racing through his camp: "Every man to his station! Fall in to attack Quebec!"

Soldiers and officers responded to the muster-call with a spirit that warmed Montgomery's heart, and it looked as if the morale which his men had shown during their best moments, at St. John's and on entering Montreal, had re-asserted itself. But the sky remained clear all day and into the evening, with no sign of clouds appearing. On a clear night the approaching Americans would be a plain target against the moonlit snow, which the defenders would see from far off. Reluctantly the general had the alert counter-manded, and the men were dismissed. Montgomery's order of the day on the twenty-eighth was circulated throughout the American camp, expressing the general's "great pleasure in seeing the good disposition with which the troops moved to the attack." He had postponed the battle in order to save lives by waiting for a more favorable opportunity, Montgomery said, promising that the action would come soon:

"It is hoped and expected that no soldier who is jealous for the success of the enterprise will absent himself from his quarters at night, as he might be called upon at a moment's warning."

Come what may, clear night or dark, Richard Montgomery knew as he issued this order of the day that he must lead his army against the walls and cannon of Fortress Quebec within another forty-eight hours.

❧ 8 ❧

Assault by Storm

THROUGH spies and deserters from the American camp, Guy Carleton had been kept well informed of Montgomery's situation since he had surrounded Quebec. The British commander knew that the Americans had received a trickling of reinforcements late in December, but that they had no hope of securing heavy artillery this season. It was obvious to him that they planned to attack the town, rather than besiege it for months. But there were two things Carleton did not know. One was the exact reason for Montgomery's anxiety to storm the city before the turn of the year. The other was his opponent's precise plan of attack.

Since it was known in the city that Montgomery had come close to launching his attack on the night of December 27th, and that only the telltale moonlight had restrained him, Carleton was doubly on the alert. The blow would doubtless come on the next dark night. Furthermore, it was evident that the Americans were suffering from exposure to the weather and from disease, while at the same time their meager supplies were being steadily consumed. Obviously, time was pressing hard on Montgomery. If he were to attack at all, he would be in a stronger position to strike sooner, rather than later. So Carleton and his garrison remained ready, from day to day and through every hour of the long winter nights.

Originally, Richard Montgomery had planned to strike the defense line around Quebec in two places simultaneously. One force was to attack the Lower Town, while the principal attack was to be directed at the wall near the southwest corner bastion, not far from the two-hundred-foot cliff overhanging the St. Lawrence. But intelligence leaks from his headquarters were cause enough for him to abandon this scheme. In addition, the snows had come down so heavily that his men would be hopelessly bogged down attempting to approach the walls across the open plain, while carrying their weapons and scaling ladders.

The plan on which he finally resolved was a complex and risky one, but it offered the best chance of success of any that the Americans could devise. There were to be two feints, or pretended attacks, against the west side of the city by relatively small parties. Moving up to the walls about an hour before dawn, the diversion forces were to attract as much of the defenders' attention as possible, in the hope that Carleton would order the bulk of his force to that part of the town in order to repel them. Both parties would carry scaling ladders, and would be backed up with mortar fire aimed at the sector of the town just within the defense walls. If possible, they would pile bundles of faggots against the city gates and set them afire.

While the two smaller parties were getting their feint attacks under way on the high ground west of the Upper Town, two strong assault forces composing the bulk of the

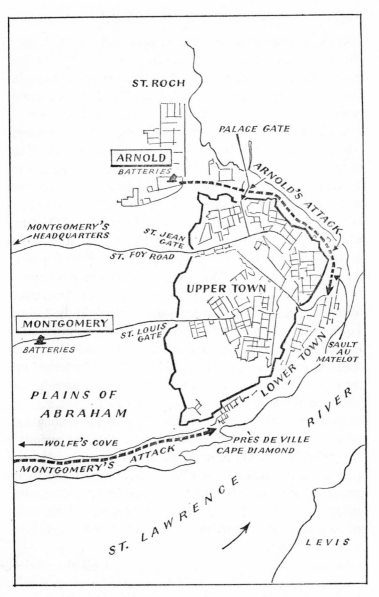

MONTGOMERY'S ATTACK ON QUEBEC

American army were to strike at both ends of the Lower Town beneath the cliffs. Montgomery hoped that these two major columns, profiting from the diversion a mile away in the upper part of the city, and from the darkness, could smash their way past whatever resistance could be encountered. The defenses here were palisades made of spar-timber, whereas everywhere else they were of solid stonework. The assault parties would charge through the streets of the Lower Town from both directions, and join forces near the foot of the Rue de La Montagne. At that point they would be in possession of the crowded, commercial section of Quebec, which contained most of its wealth and perhaps a majority of its working population, who lived in the upper floors of the three-story stone buildings that flanked its narrow streets.

Should the attack succeed as planned, the Americans would find plenty of shelter from the elements in the Lower Town, and could protect themselves easily from musket-fire. If he should choose, the governor-general could direct that the guns on the ramparts of the Upper Town be turned on the section below, and within a short time the Lower Town could be set afire and smashed into rubble. But such a cannonade would cause a grievous loss of life among the civilian population. Montgomery trusted that the majority of the Quebec men in arms in the Upper Town would prevent the commander from ruining their homes and their places of business, and slaughtering their helpless wives and children. If the militiamen would stay Carleton from such an inhuman act of war, then, he hoped, they would surrender the town.

December 28th—wind at the southwest all day. Skies clear, temperature fairly mild. Defenders on close watch through the day and the night that followed. In the American camp, Montgomery ordered a swig of rum all around to stimulate circulation and keep up cheer.

December 29th—wind swung around to the west-north-west, still clear and mild. Montgomery discussed his attack plan with a handful of key officers, with strict instructions that they be kept secret from the junior officers and men until the final assembly before the assault.

December 30th—wind from the east; the day fairly mild. But toward evening clouds began forming over the headland across the St. Lawrence, and as darkness fell the cloak of cloud moved across the sky like a death shroud. It was the signal to Montgomery and his ranking officers that tonight they must attack Quebec. Within a day they would either have brought their long, painful campaign to a glorious victory, or they would have failed. Each must have dwelt on the alternative in his own mind, though no man could tell what it might be.

Snow was falling hard early in the night as General Montgomery's staff assembled at Holland House to go over the attack plan once more. Colonel Benedict Arnold was to lead his five hundred men from the suburb of St. Roch around the north end of the city, skirting close to the walls, turn the corner, and, slipping down the rocky slope toward the waterfront wharves, was to strike the north end of the port. He was to be accompanied by Captain Lamb's company of artillery, which would drag a 3-pound brass field piece through the snow for use against the stockade. General Montgomery was to lead three hundred men along the St. Lawrence shore, and enter the Lower Town from the south. The feint attacks were to be directed by a Captain Brown, with about one hundred fifty men, against the wall near the St. Louis gate, and by a Canadian volunteer named

James Livingston, who would lead two hundred Canadians against the St. Jean gate.

For a few hours the men were permitted to rest if they could. Most of the officers, however, were busy conferring with those of the neighboring companies, and seeing to it that each sergeant and soldier checked the readiness of his firearm indoors by lamplight. Dried cartridges were passed around and secured in ammunition cases. Straps were nervously adjusted, again and again. Fresh flints were substituted for those that were worn, fireholes were cleared, barrels cleaned and fresh powder, ball and dry wadding were rammed home.

Through the hours of nervous preparation and anxious delay, as in every pre-attack wait since men first organized armies, the Americans reacted to their tension and fear in a variety of ways. Some fell silent, seeking refuge in thoughts of home and peace. Others chatted nervously, as if the very act of talking would cover their apprehension over what the next few hours would bring. There was sweat, nausea, uncontrollable urine and loose bowels—all perfectly normal manifestations of the conflict between man's instinct to preserve his life, and the grim business of marching into gunfire that spelled death.

At three in the morning the troops under Montgomery's direct leadership lined up on the St. Foy Road near Holland House. Dim lanterns, shielded against the driving snow, were carried at intervals along the line as the column moved out across the open heights, toward the ravine path that led down the cliff to Wolfe's Cove. At about the same time, Arnold's command in the suburb of St. Roch was assembled much closer to the city, yet out of musket range from the walls. Simultaneously, the two parties responsible for launching the feint attacks across the open ground directly toward the west walls were setting out into the storm.

By four o'clock in the morning, an hour when night winds usually begin to slacken in anticipation of the dawn, the heavy blasts from the east sweeping in from the St. Lawrence estuary were still as intense as ever. Driving snow directly into every man's face, into the folds of his coat on throat and chest, the wind seemed to be seeking out the hidden crevices and cracks in each soldier's defenses against the cold. The men had to lean forward, bent over like so many pack animals, in order to make progress through the howling gale. Maintaining close contact in the intensely dark night was difficult, and from the time each column set out from its starting point, it repeatedly stretched out thin in places, then came together with clashing suddenness, like a giant, serpentine-shaped accordion. Eyes closed to slits, faces muffled as tightly as possible in their scarves, soldiers repeatedly bumped into the next man's weapon, or were bruised by the soldier immediately behind, as the lines lurched forward through the darkness.

At the head of the two columns of diversion that were advancing due east toward the Quebec walls, the leading men would plunge doggedly forward into the heavy snow and try to trample out a pathway for those behind. It was slow, painful work, that exhausted a man within a few minutes, and forced him to give over the task to another. In places the trailbreakers would stumble into a drift so deep that they would sink nearly to the waist. Extricating themselves, they would back up and seek a passable route several yards to one side. In other spots they would come upon an area from which the wind had swept the loose snow almost clear, and the trail would lead easily over a hard crust into which their heels would crunch with every step.

Within two hours the hundred men under Captain Brown, who had been working their way along the exposed southern edge of the Heights of Abraham, approached their designated halting spot, not far from the edge of the St. Lawrence cliffs. Their objective was a rise of ground that lay just eighty yards from the Cape Diamond bastion. Behind a slight knoll they were offered a measure of protection from its guns. Stealthily covering the last few hundred yards, the men spread out in the snow in a skirmish line facing the fortification, which they could not quite make out through the darkness and falling snow. But they sensed its presence ahead of them like a hidden monster. Seeking protection from the gunfire that would soon be directed at them, the soldiers burrowed into the snow as best they could. As they did so, they were unaware that more than one watcher on the walls had observed the faint pinpoints of light from their shaded lanterns, that appeared from the bastion like a line of tiny, winking fireflies.

Meanwhile, more than a half mile across the snowbound plain, the column of some two hundred Canadian volunteers under Major James Livingston was coming close to the St. Jean gate. At the same time the batterymen standing by their mortars in St. Roch were anxiously looking in the direction of the Cape Diamond bastion for the attack signal —three skyrockets to be fired into the air at five o'clock.

It had not taken long for Montgomery's assault force of three hundred men to reach the cliff above Wolfe's Cove. The path to its base, once extremely rough, was now thoroughly worn by weeks of use as a supply route between the boats in the cove and the army on the heights. The party wound its way down the declivity to the shore, then, turning to the left, headed directly into the driving gale toward Quebec. On one side loomed the rocky cliffs, which hung above the column in fierce and rugged majesty—now white in patches where ice and snow had piled up in a sheltered crevice, now dark where the wall was too sheer for ice to maintain a hold. Along the right side of the narrow foot-path stretched the jumbled slabs of ice thrown up by the St. Lawrence in its last heaves of tidal power before winter had sealed it for the season. Between the rocks and the ice, the rough footway was narrow, tangled and treacherous. Time and again men stumbled and slipped as they made their way forward through the night, crashing to a hard fall on hip or knee, slamming their ribs into a protruding musket lock, cursing, freezing in face, hands and feet.

Having realized for a long time that the morale of his troops was the most doubtful factor in all his planning, Montgomery had decided that he must take his place near the head of his assault column in order to speed the men forward. A command to advance issued by a general who remained safely in the rear had a hollow, uninspiring ring to it. This every experienced officer knew. But a rallying cry of "Follow me, my boys!" or "Come on, men!", issued by a commander in the very front of the fight, would inspire ordinary men to rise above their fears and charge into danger with courage.

So it had been with Alexander and Julius Caesar, with Robert the Bruce of Scotland, with Henry V at Agincourt, with Henry of Navarre at Ivry. Richard Montgomery in the long weeks since he had determined to carry Quebec by storm must often have pondered the lesson their example had taught. None but the brave have the right to demand the bravery of those they lead. This was the true *noblesse oblige* of the gentleman at arms—the obligation to show the way, at whatever personal risk, to his subordinates.

From his place near the front of the column that now proceeded with cautious steps, Indian-file along the St. Lawrence bank, Montgomery must have turned over and over in his mind the sight that would greet him near the corner of Cape Diamond. The first defenses lay before the narrow cluster of houses called Près de Ville. Through informants who had left the city Montgomery had learned the exact plan of the barriers and strongpoints in this hamlet. James Thompson had supervised the construction of a heavy palisade of vertical timbers, about twelve to fifteen feet high and sharpened at the top. It ran part of the way up the slope at the base of the cliff on the left hand side, and down to the edge of the jumbled ice floes on the right. The pickets were stout ones, but Montgomery had brought carpenters who could probably saw them through, or pry them apart just sufficiently to permit one man at a time to slip through an opening. At least, the howling wind would tend to cover the noise they would make. In addition, the heavy piling up of snow and ice at either end of the barrier might permit one file of men to clamber around each end on top of the frozen mass.

About fifty feet beyond the first barrier another stockade of heavy timbers stretched across the gap between cliff and river. Just beyond this second defense, the final projection of rocks from the cliff base fell back to the left, away from the shoreline, and led directly to the nearest of the permanent stone houses, perhaps one hundred feet down the pathway. Here, under the shelter of the cliff, Thompson had erected a solid blockhouse of heavy logs, with firing loopholes for riflemen in the ground floor and two medium fieldpieces in the upper story. Diagonally across from the blockhouse, close to the river's edge, stood a solid building that normally was used as a potash works, but which had been transformed since the siege began into a guardhouse. Beside it stood two more cannon, facing the inside of the innermost timber barricade, and a fifth cannon was placed not far away. The upper windows of several houses along the narrow roadway behind the blockhouse had been boarded up to serve as protected positions for riflemen.

Whether there had been any further defenses put in here in the past few weeks to strengthen this narrow strip of the Lower Town, Montgomery did not know. But provided they could penetrate the timber stockades under cover of darkness and the projecting point of rock from the cliff, the only possible tactic would be a bold charge in defiance of the opening blast of the guns. With luck, they might surprise the gunners before they could fire, or frighten them into flight or surrender. At worst, a dozen or two men would fall, but enough could then race forward past them to seize the gun positions before the defenders would have time to swab out their pieces and reload. This was the chance that those in front would have to take. Their fate would be in the hand of God.

Montgomery's column was still several hundred yards short of its objective, and the lead scout at the head of the column had not yet sighted the first barricade, when the commander's watch showed that it was almost five o'clock. The time for attack was almost upon them. The word was passed back down the line of the approach march to hurry, and officers speeded their men forward by muttered commands. Already the first light of day was beginning to penetrate the night, and almost without having noticed it the troops realized that they could now see several paces ahead. With the tentative approach of dawn the snowfall slacked off somewhat, and the wind eased in force. Almost too soon daylight was approaching.

Suddenly, to his surprise and horror, Richard Montgomery heard one shot from somewhere above his left shoulder, then several more. The sky flashed bright near the top of Cape Diamond in the glare of a rocket. The signal to attack had been fired. It was too soon—before his column had even reached the Près de Ville barrier! Now they must rush forward without caution, just as fast as they could, and get through the first defenses before they would be discovered. Turning and shouting encouragement to the troops within sound of his voice, Montgomery led the assault force toward the stockade athwart his way into Quebec.

Three hundred feet above Montgomery's struggling column, the ramparts on the Cape Diamond headland confronted Captain Brown's party. As the sentinels paced the walls and peered out into the snowy night with the wind at their backs, they had the advantage of seeing more clearly than the approaching Americans, whose vision was impeded by the cold wind and snow. When Captain Malcolm Fraser of the corps of Royal Emigrants, who was serving as captain of the guard from sundown on December 30th to morning of the 31st, reached this part of the west defenses, a sentry told him of the dots of light he had seen somewhat earlier. Fraser was instantly on the alert, since this was the hour when an attack could most be expected, and this had been the kind of dark night most favoring the enemy's approach.

Suddenly all doubt was dispelled. A bright light was fired

into the sky from somewhere out in front of him, then a second, and a third. Skyrockets! A signal for attack! It could mean nothing else. Captain Fraser ran shouting along the wall, down the stairs to the ground by the St. Louis gate, then across the open space behind the walls to St. Louis Street and along it into the Upper Town.

"Turn out! Turn out!" Fraser shouted. "Attack on Cape Diamond! To your posts! To your posts!"

The cries of alarm rang through the town, street to street, house to house. In every dwelling heavy wooden shutters and doors, thrown open for a moment to receive the news, were banged shut to protect those inside from musket fire and shell fragments. Men who had been sleeping in their clothes for nights on end struggled into their coats and ran through the streets to their defense positions. Lighted torches appeared from doorways and were seen bobbing their way through the dark, carried aloft jerkily by excited militia-men. French cries of warning mingled with English shouts. Over all could be heard the bells of every church and public building in the city, clanging and becoming the alarm signal in a dozen jarring tones.

Within a few minutes General Carleton was roused at his command post in the Franciscan seminary. Told of the direction from which the first alarm had come, he ordered some units to the walls in that quarter. In the meantime, immediately after the attack signals had been sent into the night sky over Cape Diamond, the Americans began to blaze away with their muskets toward the ramparts, creating exactly the kind of diversion which Montgomery had planned. The defenders shot a few of their cannon in the general direction of the musket-fire, but in the darkness could not tell how much damage they had inflicted.

A full mile to the north, from the cluster of buildings that made up the St. Roch suburb, intermittent bursts of mortar fire began a new diversion to cover the approach of Livingston's Canadian volunteers toward the St. Jean gate. As mortar shells crashed into the northwest sector of the Upper Town, the defenders who manned the walls in this quarter found themselves likewise under a fusillade. They responded with grapeshot from the cannon, and in order to prevent a scaling party from reaching the walls unobserved they set a number of fireballs alight and heaved them over the parapets. The snow engulfed some of the spluttering flares. But those that remained on the hard, icy surface where they fell cast a flickering glow far enough to give the Quebec forces assurance against surprise. Shouting from the defiant attack force and spasmodic firing continued, but it was evident before long that a serious attack was not under way on this part of the Quebec defense perimeter.

Some minutes before Captain Brown's signal flares mounted into the sky, Benedict Arnold had set his long attack column in motion from the north edge of the city. While the first shouts of alarm were sounding faintly from the streets and houses beyond the walls that hovered over the St. Roch and Palais suburbs, Arnold's men were already dodging rapidly along at the base of the rocky slope beneath the defense wall, skirting the very edge of the town. The icy and snowy ground was rough here, but Arnold and his followers had the advantage of proceeding downhill. They dashed from the shelter of one building to another, slipping and sliding, joining in bunches for a few moments, then alternately running and stalking as they moved along the flank of the town. In each man's throat was an unspoken prayer that he would not be seen from the walls above his right shoulder.

But this was too much to ask. The entire town was in clamor and on the alert in all directions. Almost in a moment they were discovered. Arnold's leading companies found themselves spotlighted against the snow—perfect targets illuminated by flares tossed down upon them from the parapet. With a deadly staccato sound, muskets and rifles opened fire on them from the walls above. For more than two hundred yards each man was forced to run a gauntlet of fire, to which he could pause to reply only at his mortal peril. One figure after another began to fall into the snowy pathway, to be bypassed by his comrades racing for the shelter of the first stone buildings of the Lower Town, that could be seen just a few yards ahead.

Yet on they came, one after another, some lumbering heavily along in twos and threes hauling the scaling ladders and the tools with which to breach the barricade at the near end of the street. Captain Lamb's artillery piece proved a hopeless burden. Too heavy to be carried down the steep approach to the Lower Town, too awkward to be hauled by sledge between heavy blocks of ice while fire rained down on the artillerymen, it was abandoned in the snow. Company after company of riflemen followed in the path of the leading elements, which had already attained the wooden barrier that sealed off Sault au Matelot, the single street at this end of the town, built on the strip of land between the overhanging rocky cliff to the right and the waterfront wharves on the river side.

Sault au Matelot, Canadian French for "Sailor's Leap," had been named long years before, as Quebec legend held, to mark the spot where a seaman had leaped over the precipice of Quebec to his death on the rocks below. Others believed the name came from the fact that here is where sailors jumped ashore from their vessels, happy to return to their home port. Whatever the real origin of its name, Sault au Matelot had become a busy commercial street, close to three hundred yards long, narrowly confined between high stone houses, each built directly touching its neighbors. At the north end the street opened on the shore side to Limburner's Wharf. At its south end, that farthest from the palisade confronting the American assault force, it led directly into the Rue de la Montagne, the twisting road to the Upper Town. At this far end, as well, the engineering workers under Superintendent Thompson had built a second wooden palisade, protected by a couple of light cannon on a raised platform attached to its rear face. Midway in Sault au Matelot the street and its flanking houses bent at a slight angle, just sufficiently that the guns from the inner defense barricade would not aim directly at the rear of the outer one, nor could they sweep the street in its entire length.

The Americans advanced rapidly upon the first barricade. Before the defenders were in a position to open fire with their muskets and cannon, the attackers were directly in front of them, yelling defiance like wild Indians and firing as they advanced. Within a few seconds the Americans had the psychological advantage, as the defenders hesitated between returning fire or running for safety. Only one of the guns was set off, badly aimed and doing minimal damage, as the Americans threw their ladders against the palisade and swarmed over the top to gain the firing parapet within. The leader was Captain Daniel Morgan, a veteran Indian fighter from Virginia, who had followed General Washington to Boston, and thence had gone with Arnold through the Maine wilderness to Quebec. A rough, tough, single-minded hater of British authority, Morgan had been the logical choice of Benedict Arnold to take over command of the attack when a musket ball fired from the parapet above had torn into Arnold's left calf and severely crippled him. While Arnold was making his way back to the hospital, chagrined at his ill fortune and bleeding heavily from his wound, Morgan and his riflemen were followed over the barricade by a steady swarm of Americans, eager for the kill.

Taken by surprise, and chilled by the fear of being slaughtered on the spot, the Quebec militiamen and British regulars hurried from their guardhouses adjoining the barricade and threw down their arms in surrender. Morgan ordered them to be herded together and held under guard, while he went forward with the advance elements that had already gained the Sault au Matelot. Behind him one hundred Americans entered the street, then a second hundred, and a third. As they moved forward, partially shielded by the high buildings from direct fire from the upper ramparts, an occasional shot teased them from house windows toward the far end of the barricaded street. The Americans turned the slight angle of Sault au Matelot, faced directly into the far barricade and charged through the icy street toward this objective.

By this time, however, the defending gunners and marksmen were ready, having been prepared by the alarms and firing that had occupied the past twenty or thirty minutes. With a roar the guns spewed their metal shot down the narrow alleyway of Sault au Matelot. Halted in their tracks, the Continental soldiers resembled so many tottering tenpins. A dozen fell into the snow and lay still. A few dragged themselves, trailing blood in their tracks, into the nearest doorways opening to the street. The men who were not wounded smashed their way through windows and doorways to find shelter from the lethal guns. Now the defenders were in control, and the foremost attackers were scattered, caught in small groups inside the houses. Their momentum had been halted. The wounded, crying out for aid, lay helpless in the icebound street among the dead. At the north end of the street a large group of apprehensive Quebec prisoners were huddled together in the open, held under guard by a few Americans who were asking themselves whether they could hold their ground if the tide should turn.

At his command post in the Upper Town, Guy Carleton began to fit together the pieces of information that were relayed to him by messengers close to the various scenes of action. The rising light of morning showed the officers facing the plain to the west of town that they had little to fear from that quarter. Brown's and Livingston's parties were of nuisance value only, and their shooting toward the walls was becoming less and less frequent. It seemed apparent now that the most serious attack was that coming into the Lower Town from the north. Four of five companies, or perhaps six, must have run beneath the defenses, and a goodly toll of these had been taken in the firing from the ramparts.

But suddenly it appeared to Carleton that these attackers had put themselves in a position to be struck from the rear. No more of them could be seen running forward past the points of observation on the northeast edge of the Quebec defenses. The wounded and the frightened could be seen retreating back toward the suburbs. If the Americans were holding any forces in reserve, they could not be many. Nonetheless, Carleton was extremely hesitant to abandon his cardinal rule, which the defeat of Montcalm had impressed upon him: that if the enemy cannot get through a defense perimeter, do not play the fool and sortie from it. For a full month the stout walls and artillery of Fortress Quebec had been his protective shield. Should he take a chance now, and leave this protection to strike a blow in the open?

Messengers brought in the news that the attackers had been stopped at the inner barricade and were caught in the narrow Sault au Matelot. Hesitating no longer, Carleton ordered three parties of reliable men to leave the fortifications by the Palace Gate. They were to follow in the very same path that the attackers had taken more than an hour before, to swing around to the entry of the Lower Town, flushing out the enemy as they went, and then seal off the assault force from the rear. In a relatively short time two hundred men had left the sally port and were advancing on the unsuspecting Morgan and his stalled, divided assault force.

As the trap was being closed upon him, Morgan rallied his men for a determined attack on the upper barricade. For some minutes there was desperate fighting in the houses close to the barrier, as attackers and defenders fired from window to window at one another, and from upper windows down into the gun platform behind the defense works. Bit by bit the Americans were picked off, their numbers reduced. Their spirit flagged as one man after another fell.

Where, the surviving fighters wanted to know, was Montgomery's column? Why were the general's men not striking at the barrier from the rear, so they could clear it away and join forces?

Minutes passed, then an hour, and with it the final chance for Morgan's party to clear the street that had turned from his conquest to his conqueror. By the time he had given the

order, with sinking heart, that his men should withdraw
from Sault au Matelot, the British had sealed off their escape
route from the rear. The herd of Quebec prisoners, suddenly released as their comrades poured over the northern
barricade, grabbed weapons and turned them on their former
guards. Hemmed in on all sides by superior numbers, unable
to advance, blocked from retreat, flushed from their refuges
in houses along the street, the Americans were disarmed.

After two hours of explosion and gunsmoke, the sound
of shattering glass, the whine of bullets and piteous cries of
the terrified wounded, all grew still along Quebec's street of
death. The falling snow had already obliterated the blood-
stains of the first to be torn by lead and iron. It fell now on
the bodies of a hundred soldiers scattered along the route of
Arnold's and Morgan's assault, all the way from the edge
of the St. Roch suburb to the Sault au Matelot barrier, and
along the length of the street to within a few yards of the
Rue de la Montagne. They had come almost within reach
of their goal, but it had eluded their grasp.

Where was Montgomery?

The attack signal had been fired when he was several
hundred yards short of his first objective, the palisade across
the pathway leading into the hamlet of Près de Ville. The
column hurried forward, under the fear of being discovered
to their disadvantage, and within a few minutes those in the
lead had come in sight of the timber barrier. There was no
sound from behind it, and no lights anywhere to indicate
the presence of guards. The wind sweeping in diagonally
from the river was proving a friend, for it acted so as to
overcome the sounds of alarm that were arousing the Upper
Town.

Skirting as close to the cliff as possible to take advantage of whatever camouflage and protection it would afford, Montgomery and about twenty others crept up to the palisade. Still no sound, and no challenge. Eager hands were quickly at work, sawing through three or four of the vertical spars, and a doorway was soon opened through this outer line of defense. Hearts pounding in anticipation, breath constricted against whatever might strike at them in the snowy gloom, Richard Montgomery and his vanguard slipped through the opening and crouched in the rocky recesses at the base of the cliff. Still they heard nothing, and no light showed ahead. Were they being watched? Or were they still undiscovered?

Whispered instructions passed down the column. Come forward! Through the breach! Quietly, quietly! Hold your weapons close to the body and keep down! Bring the men up as quickly as possible!

Yard by yard, creeping close in the shadow of the Cape Diamond rocks, the forward party covered the few dozen yards toward the second barrier, reached it and began to saw into the timbers of the end close to the cliff. Still, as they peered anxiously through the cracks, they could see no sentries and hear no sound of anyone stirring. Was it possible that Près de Ville was still asleep? Had the roar of the wind, the muffling effect of the snow, and the great height of the Cape Diamond cliff kept anyone here from seeing any lights from the Upper Town, or hearing any sounds of alarm?

In a few more minutes the second barrier's timbers yielded to saw and crowbar. Again, a doorway had been cut large enough for a man to pass easily with his pack and weapon. Montgomery stepped through it, along with his volunteer engineer from Quebec, Edward Antill, his aide de camp, Captain John MacPherson, the general's orderly sergeant, Captain Jacob Cheeseman, and about twelve others. Behind them a hundred or more of the troops had reached the first barrier or had already passed it.

Cautiously one of the party sneaked forward a few paces to the jutting corner of the cliff, that hid them from the blockhouse standing guard over the entry to Près de Ville. He was back in an instant, to report noise of activity from within the buildings, and lights appearing in a number of windows. The alarm had reached the guard post.

With the instinct of one who sees the opportunity of a moment that will not come again, Montgomery turned to those behind and shouted in his most commanding voice:

"Forward! Men of New York! Quebec is ours!"

Then, as one man after another passed the break in the stockade and followed him, the general turned the corner of rock and ran forward toward the blockhouse at the head of the street, and the city of Quebec which lay beyond it.

The Près de Ville defense post had been built in such a solid manner, and the pathway between the cliffs and shore were considered by Carleton and his officers such an unlikely route for an attack, that Près de Ville was not heavily manned. In command was a Captain Chabotte of the French Canadian militia, with fewer than forty men under his orders. Supporting him, however, was a British ship's captain named Barnsfare, with nine British seamen-gunners and an experienced sergeant of the Royal Artillery. The two stockades under Cape Diamond were so stoutly built, and the blockhouse in such an advantageous position to sweep the open place of fifty or more paces ahead of it, that the defenders apparently felt no need to place sentinels forward of these defenses.

The alarm signal had, indeed, carried to the men on guard at the Près de Ville post, both by flashing lights and the sound of shouts and bells. From somewhere up above, in the distance, they could hear the first firing of the battle. While Montgomery's vanguard was at the first palisade and his carpenters were at work, Captains Chabotte and Barnsfare were making ready for action. Within the blockhouse close to the guns a fire of coals, buried deep under the ashes of early morning, was blown into life. Fuses were pushed into the fireholes of the cannon. The artillery sergeant stood ready with slow-match lighted. Militiamen and sailors, French and British, peered from their firing ports gripping their muskets, as they made out the first shadowy figures of the enemy clustered by the rocks.

There was a pause, as Captain Barnsfare calmly surveyed the ground before him, motioning to the gunners to hold their fire. Was this a sneak party of reconnaissance, a handful of men who would run for their lives on the first shot? Or were they part of a large assault force? No one in the blockhouse could see any but these first few men, dimly silhouetted through the falling snow.

Suddenly Barnsfare's order rang out in a voice of thunder: "Fire! Fire! Reload and fire!"

Lighted match caught the powder of the fuse, which spluttered brightly for a few seconds as the men stood back, hands over ears in expectation. The naval cannon crashed, and jerked violently back against its restraining ropes. The gunroom of the blockhouse filled with choking smoke. Muskets in the room below resounded with continued fire, and were joined by others shot by marksmen placed in vantage points outside. For a full minute the shooting continued until nothing was seen stirring in the snow-covered yard between the timber barrier, the blockhouse and the potash works at the edge of the river.

An hour later, the dim, gray light of a winter's morning revealed a dozen bodies sprawled where they had fallen in the snow. Not another enemy figure appeared for hour after hour, though the Près de Ville garrison stood cautious and ready to repulse a second assault. In the early afternoon the sky darkened and the snowfall became heavier. It continued steadily as the day passed, the day that marked the end of the old year, as if to seal over with white the scenes of blood and fear that the year 1775 had brought to Quebec. By nightfall the bodies still lay where they had fallen, and were almost covered in an icy shroud.

❧ 9 ❧

"A Humane and Generous Rebel"

ON New Year's Day the snow that had been falling on Quebec for thirty-six hours finally stopped. The garrison had spent the night before on a sharp alert, apprehensive lest whatever remained of the American army make one more desperate strike against the city. But all remained quiet as the old year passed into history. Seventeen-seventy-six dawned with the Union Jack of Great Britain still flying over Fortress Quebec. About its ramparts and within, the fresh snowfall, soft, deep and glistening white, had obliterated almost every evidence of the battle.

Venturing from their buildings on the morning of January 1st, the guards at Près de Ville went forward to examine the barricade that they had defended during the attack, and from which three hundred of the enemy had retreated in confusion when their leaders were shot down. From the snow in the open space that they had raked with fire Captain Barnsfare and his men uncovered thirteen frozen bodies. One of them, wounded in three places by grapeshot fired from the cannon in the blockhouse, was that of an officer who, by the fine quality of his dress and the fact that he carried a sword and pocket watch, was thought to be the corpse of General Richard Montgomery.

An officer was brought from among those taken prisoner to identify the bodies where they lay on the snow. The captive officer needed but one look to confirm the identity of his dead general. Stricken with grief at the sight, he pointed out to the defenders of the Près de Ville gate the bodies of Montgomery, Captain John MacPherson, Captain Cheeseman, the general's orderly-sergeant and several of the others. Then he carried the disheartening news of Montgomery's death back to the other prisoners, many of whom wept unashamedly for the loss of their leader. While an American army still stood before Quebec, they had hoped that they might somehow be rescued. But now that they knew Montgomery was dead, the American prisoners could see little chance either for the depleted army or for themselves. The picture of Ethan Allen, shipped to England in chains, loomed before their eyes.

Although he had vanquished the enemy who had caused him endless pain and frustration, General Guy Carleton was unwilling to treat Montgomery, even in death, with the dignity of a fellow-officer. Just as he had made a point to show scorn for him in life, Carleton would make no concessions to "Mr. Montgomery," the dead rebel. It was left to Lieutenant-Governor Cramahé to bury Richard Montgomery like a Christian gentleman. On the night of January 3rd, Cramahé and a handful of Quebec citizens took part in a quiet graveside ceremony held by torchlight in an obscure corner of a garden in the Upper Town. There were no honors of war, no procession, no public signs of respect, not even a representative from among the captured American officers.

Thus were interred the mortal remains of the commanding general of the American forces at Quebec, the third
leader of an army within a generation to meet his death in
battle for possession of that fortress. General Wolfe's body
had been borne home to England to rest amid his own people. Montcalm, buried in the Ursuline convent in Quebec,
would be among his countrymen as long as men would speak
French in the province he defended. But Montgomery's remains were destined to lie for many years far from his family, friends and home. Yet there were those, even among the
forces that had defeated him, who recognized his talents
and his virtues. One English gentleman who had been active in the defense of Quebec wrote in his journal under the
date of January 1st, 1776:

"A genteel coffin is ordered by the Lieutenant Governor
for the interment of Mr. Montgomery. Those who knew him
formerly in this place sincerely lament his late infatuation.
They say he was a genteel man, and an agreeable com-
panion."

General Guy Carleton remained cautiously on the defensive. Successful so far with this strategy, he would not
risk sending his troops out into the heavy snow in pursuit
of the Americans who had withdrawn from the battle when
they saw it was lost. Conservative by his nature, Carleton
tended to exaggerate the number of men still in the American camp, believing they totaled nearly one thousand. In
actual fact they were a scant four hundred, plus a couple of
hundred Canadian volunteers whose spirit was greatly weak-
ened by the defeat in which Montgomery fell. Carleton could
count more than four hundred Americans either dead or
taken prisoner in the assault, and he could presume that a
good many more were lying ill or wounded in the enemy

camp. But he did not realize that the Americans had lost half their effective force in the fateful attack. His own force, all told, had suffered fewer than forty men in killed and wounded. It made good sense to Carleton to tighten his defenses, not risk a sortie, and let disease, cold and despair continue working in his behalf against these men who had lost their one capable leader.

In one respect the British general relented somewhat in his stern attitude toward these rebels who opposed him. He permitted a representative of the officers taken prisoner with Captain Daniel Morgan's corps to leave the city and arrange for their personal baggage to be brought to them under a flag of truce. In showing this kindness to the officers in captivity, and later in allowing them to be inoculated against smallpox by a Quebec surgeon, and again in agreeing to let their personal letters be sent out to their families, he won the regard of a number of the American prisoners as a more humane captor than he had formerly seemed as an opponent.

At the request of Colonel Benedict Arnold, who assumed command of the Continentals after his wounded leg was dressed, Carleton sent Montgomery's pocket watch to Holland House by a messenger, for eventual return to the dead general's family. But in his report to his military superior in North America, General Howe, Guy Carleton held to his pose of dismissing Montgomery with disdain. His opponent, he wrote, had led an attack that was "soon repulsed, with slaughter. Mr. Montgomery was left among the dead."

Because Richard Montgomery was the first officer of high rank in the Continental army to be killed in the war, his death deeply affected the leaders of the gathering American

Revolution. General Washington received the news of Mont-gomery's defeat and death on January 18th in a melancholy letter from Philip Schuyler. He, in turn, had received word from Arnold by way of General Wooster at Montreal. The commander in chief wrote to Schuyler in reply:

> "I am heartily sorry, and most sincerely condole with you upon the unhappy fall of the brave and worthy Montgomery, and those gallant officers and men who have experienced a like fate.
> "In the death of this gentleman, America has sus-tained a heavy loss, as he had proved himself a steady friend to her rights, and of ability to render her the most essential service."

Schuyler's letter had been especially shocking to General Washington because the commander in chief was so desper-ately short of munitions with which to oppose the British army at Boston that he had written directly to Montgomery, as recently as January 12th, urgently asking for supplies from the military stores in Quebec. Powder, arms, blankets, clothing—"whatever you can spare, we shall have occasion for," General Washington had urged Montgomery.

> "Your sending them as expeditiously as possible will be doing vast service to this Army, and very much oblige, sir, yours,
>
> *George Washington*."

The commander in chief had addressed his letter of Jan-uary 12th to "Major-General Richard Montgomery, Can-ada." Isolated by the Quebec winter, Montgomery had never received word of this promotion. But General Washington and the rest of the country had learned that the Continental Congress had promoted Montgomery from brigadier to major general on December 9th, in recognition of his victorious leadership of the army in Canada. In fact, Montgomery's were the only genuine victories that the Continental army had won during the six months since its organization. At the turn of 1776, the name of General Richard Montgomery was more widely known and genuinely revered than any other in the United Colonies, save only that of General Washington himself.

It was therefore with the most profound sorrow that President John Hancock of the Continental Congress on January 17th read to the delegates Schuyler's message that began:

> "My amiable and gallant friend, General Montgomery, is no more. He fell in an unsuccessful attack on Quebec on the 30th ultimo. My feelings on this unhappy occasion are too poignant to admit of expression. May Heaven avert any further evils."

Members of the Continental Congress agreed with General Wooster's characterization of Montgomery—"one of the bravest men of the age"—as he described the fallen hero in a message that Schuyler forwarded to President Hancock. What proper tribute, the delegates asked themselves, could they pay to his memory? How could the example of his sacrifice, the greatest than man can offer his fellow man, serve to inspire his countrymen in the glorious cause of liberty? The Congress at length agreed to a resolution recorded in its minutes as follows:

> "Resolved, that, to express the veneration of the United Colonies for their late general, Richard Mont-

gomery, and the deep sense they entertain of the many
signal and important services of that gallant officer,
who, after a series of successes, amidst the most discouraging difficulties, fell at length in a gallant attack
upon Quebec, the capital of Canada;

"And for transmitting to future ages, as examples
truly worthy of imitation, his patriotism, conduct, boldness of enterprise, insuperable perseverance, and contempt of danger and death, a monument be procured
from Paris, or any other part of France, with an in-
scription sacred to his memory, and expressive of his
amiable character and heroic achievements;

"And that the continental treasurers be directed to
advance a sum, not exceeding £300 sterling, to Dr.
Benjamin Franklin (who is desired to see this resolution properly executed) for defraying the expense
thereof."

As the early months of the fateful year 1776 passed with
the hostilities between the British government and the United
Colonies becoming irreconcilable, the figure of Richard
Montgomery, rebel of 1775, was raised before the American
people as a rallying symbol. Popular ballads and poems told
of Montgomery's glorious campaign into Canada, and his
heroic death in the cause of liberty. Printed broadsides carrying the words were circulated from one end of the colonies
to the other. Tom Paine, the revolutionary-pamphleteer,
wrote an inspirational elegy in which the spirit of Montgomery called on patriots to follow him into the fight.
Wherever men gathered during the dark early months of the
war, before the tide turned in favor of the Continental army,
General Montgomery was held up as the hero whom patriots
should emulate when the struggle seemed hopeless.

In Great Britain, Montgomery's death at Quebec was felt

as a distressing loss to those friends who had known him since his boyhood in Ireland. It was particularly so among the Whigs and other liberal thinkers who sympathized with the colonists in their resistance to tyranny from the British Ministry. Three prominent members of the House of Commons opposition to Lord North's government, Isaac Barré, Edmund Burke and Charles James Fox, eulogized Montgomery in the House on March 11, 1776. The news of his death and the repulse of the assault on Quebec had arrived in London a few days before. In the midst of debate on the war appropriation planned by Lord North's ministry, Barré pointed with dismay to the huge cost of Britain's war in Canada, which was still a defensive operation, in contrast to the lower cost of great victories that British armies had won on the continent of Europe a few years before, when Mr. Pitt had been Prime Minister. General Montgomery had fought brilliantly, he said, and was a commander to be admired.

Edmund Burke, who had for years argued vainly in the House of Commons in opposition to Britain's use of force against the American colonies, then added to Barré's praise of Montgomery:

He was brave, he was able, he was humane, and he was generous. What is more, Montgomery before his death conquered two-thirds of Canada in one campaign.

Charles James Fox then carried on the eulogy of Montgomery, until Lord North rose in anger to reply. The Prime Minister denounced what he termed "this unqualified liberality of praise bestowed on General Montgomery by the gentlemen in opposition, because they were bestowing it on a rebel.

"I cannot join in lamenting his death as a public loss,"

said Lord North. "I will admit, indeed, that Montgomery was brave, he was able, he was humane, he was generous. But still he was only a brave, able, humane and generous rebel! One might apply to him that verse from the tragedy of Cato of ancient Rome:

" 'Curse on his virtues; they've undone his country!' "

Arising a second time, Fox replied:

"The term 'rebel,' when applied by the noble lord to that excellent person, Richard Montgomery, is no certain mark of disgrace, and therefore I am the less earnest to clear him of that imputation. For all the great asserters of liberty, the saviors of their country, the benefactors of mankind, in all ages, have been called rebels." Fox reminded his listeners that the members of the House of Commons owed their own constitution, which enabled them to take their seats in that house, to a rebellion in the previous century.

Through a long, cold winter, Arnold's feeble forces outside Quebec stayed in position, and occasionally made a show of throwing a few artillery shells into the town. But the five thousand reinforcements that he thought were required for a decisive attack on Carleton never arrived. Late in the spring, when the ice broke in the St. Lawrence and British ships sailed up to the fortress with fresh provisions, men and ammunition, Arnold and Wooster realized that they must withdraw. Within a few weeks they had retreated up the St. Lawrence Valley, then the Sorel River, giving back to the British military every square mile of the province of Quebec that Montgomery's army had occupied the previous autumn. By the end of June, the Continentals had fallen back all the way to Fort Ticonderoga, and Canada was once again completely in the hands of Governor-General Guy Carleton and his forces.

In later years, as the invasion of Canada in 1775 was seen in full perspective, it was judged a success even though Quebec City had not been taken. Montgomery's offensive had prevented the British army from using the chain of forts and the Sorel-Champlain-Hudson waterways as a route by which to invade New York and isolate the Continental forces in New England. By pinning down General Carleton in the province of Quebec for a year, Montgomery had prevented his coming to the aid of Generals Gage and Howe in Boston. The enemy had been compelled to deploy its forces excessively, with the result that in the spring of 1776 Howe was forced to the decision to evacuate Boston. The invasion of Canada, therefore, played a major part in securing New England for the Revolution.

If, on the other hand, Montgomery had taken Quebec, how would that have changed the course of the war? Would it have been won more easily? Would Quebec have become part of the United Colonies, and later of the United States? The speculation continued for years, although to no useful purpose.

Montgomery's strategic ideas on the defense of New York proved highly accurate through the eight years during which the Continentals and the redcoats faced each other as enemies. The town of New York, as he knew, could not be defended against any strong attack by British soldiers and ships of war. The British occupied the city in the fall of 1776 with little difficulty after defeating Washington on Long Island. Supported by a strong force of Hessian mercenaries, the redcoats then moved northward up Manhattan Island, taking successively the several fortified points on the high ground that were originally designed to protect the city's contact by road with the surrounding country. The last of the battles on the island was that of November 16, 1776, for Fort Washington, which had been built on the site above the Blue Bell Tavern that Montgomery had noticed on his way to the New York Congress. General Washington, who had only just left the strongpoint to be held by a rear guard, observed the battle from the palisades on the New Jersey shore of the Hudson River.

The British army held New York City throughout the rest of the war. But despite their strength in men and ships of war, they were never able to penetrate the American defenses in the Hudson Highlands, which lay some sixty miles north of the city. As Montgomery had counseled, a log and chain boom was stretched across the Hudson River at this point, covered by batteries on the heights. One of the forts here, not far from where Janet and her family lived throughout the war, was named Fort Montgomery in his honor.

It stands as one of the grand ironies of history that the commander of the American defense forces in the Hudson Highlands, who plotted unsuccessfully with the British in 1780 to betray this defense point to them, was the same Benedict Arnold who had performed so capably at the beginning of the war. Energetic and eager, brave and persevering when the American Revolution was in its infancy, Arnold's strong qualities were undermined by his boundless egotism. Because, in later years, he thought that General Washington and the Congress had been slighting him, and disregarding his talents, he turned to betrayal as a means of justifying himself. When his plot was discovered, Arnold escaped to England, where he lived out his life in obscurity.

But his name lives on in America, coupled in infamy with that of Judas Iscariot as the very symbol of betrayal. The British spy with whom Arnold conferred, Major John André, was caught by the Continental army, tried and hanged. By coincidence, it was not the first time that André had been a prisoner of the Americans; he had been among the British officers captured at St. John's when Montgomery had taken its surrender in November of 1775.

When the War for American Independence finally came to an end, General Guy Carleton was the British commander in New York. In November of 1783 Carleton, representing what was left of a defeated army and government in New York, conferred with General Washington at the outskirts of the city to arrange with the victorious American leader the orderly evacuation of the British occupation troops as Washington's forces entered. Washington was impressed with Carleton's good will and dignity in what must have been, for a proud man, a time of humiliation and of emotional stress. The American general later paid tribute to the courtesy and cooperation shown him by this last representative of the British crown with whom he was to deal before he laid down his sword. He did so late in 1783, as he had promised the New York Congress he would do in June of 1775.

On August 30th of that earlier year, while at Crown Point before entering Canada, Richard Montgomery had drawn up his last will and testament. In it he left to his sister in Ireland, Lady Ranelagh, the land and buildings at King's Bridge and other property that he owned in Ireland. "My dear sister's family," the testament said, "want all that I can spare. I could wish to recommend one or two of her youngest children to my Janet's protection.

"To my dear wife, Janet Montgomery, I give my furniture, farm utensils, carriages of all sorts, horses, cattle, shares, books, watch, mathematical and philosophical instruments and apparatus. I also leave to my said wife the farm I purchased from Shaver at Rhinebeck, with horses and everything upon it. The ample fortune which my wife will succeed to makes it unnecessary to provide for her in a manner suitable to her situation in life and adequate to the warm affection I bear her. . . .

"My brothers, whom I greatly esteem and respect, will accept of what alone I have in my power to give, my earnest wishes for their happiness!"

Upon his death Montgomery's will was forwarded, as he had requested to his brother-in-law Robert, whom he had named his executor. The personal articles in his field baggage at Holland House were inventoried on the spot, most of them were sold to the surviving officers, and the proceeds sent to his family. With the money were sent his small field library, which included, along with several books of military tactics and Roman history in French and Latin, a copy of Samuel Johnson's *Dictionary of the English Language*.

Settling Montgomery's estate required several years because of the disruptions of wartime, and many more years passed before Janet Montgomery was awarded by Congress what she considered a suitable payment to the widow of the first general officer to fall in the armed service of his country. Proud of her position as the widow of a national hero— "my general," as she referred to Richard Montgomery— Janet lived out her years in the Livingston domain of Dutchess County, somewhat withdrawn and aloof from the new society that was rapidly expanding about her. She never remarried. As the years passed she saw one after another of the United States of America and its territories name counties and towns * in honor of her husband.

In 1818, when Mrs. Montgomery was seventy-four years of age, after a second war between America and Great Britain had passed into history, it seemed fitting that the country for whose freedom he had died should be the final resting place for the first notable hero of the War for Independence. On behalf of the general's widow, Governor De Witt Clinton of New York State arranged with Sir John Sherbrooke, the Governor-General of Canada, for the return to New York of the remains of Richard Montgomery. The exact spot of burial, still unmarked, was located in a grassy plot within the walls of the Quebec Citadel, which had been built well after the Revolutionary War siege as protection against attack that never came again to the old city on the St. Lawrence. An elderly man who had been a member of the burial party forty-three years before located Montgomery's unmarked grave site for the exhumation party.

Transported to Albany under the personal supervision of Lewis Livingston, a nephew of Janet Livingston Montgomery, Montgomery's coffin was borne into the Capitol on July 4th, 1818, where it lay in state until July 6th. Then it was placed on board the steamboat *Richmond* and carried down the Hudson River toward New York City. Asking that she be left unattended on her front veranda on the morning of July 8th, Janet Livingston Montgomery was alone with her memories for a while as the steamer passed slowly down the Hudson before her eyes, carrying her general home, at last, to rest among his countrymen. When members of the

---

* There are counties named Montgomery in these states: Alabama, Arkansas, Georgia, Illinois, Indiana, Iowa, Kansas, Kentucky, Maryland, Mississippi, Missouri, New York, North Carolina, Ohio, Pennsylvania and Virginia. The capital city of Alabama is also named Montgomery.

family joined her some time later, they found she had fainted, apparently overcome by emotion.

With solemn, impressive ceremony, Montgomery's remains were interred later that day in St. Paul's Chapel of Trinity Parish, beneath the monument that had been ordered by the Continental Congress long before, when America was in its hour of deepest trial. It can be seen there today against the east wall, an oasis of quiet amid the bustle of the downtown New York financial district, where Broadway comes together with Fulton, Church and Vesey streets. The monument, carved from Pyrenees marble, was the work of the Italian sculptor Caffieri. On its face the visitor can read these words, chosen by Benjamin Franklin:

"This monument is erected by order of Congress, 25th January 1776, to transmit to posterity a grateful remembrance of the patriotic conduct, enterprise and perseverance of Major-General Richard Montgomery, who after a series of successes, amidst the most discouraging difficulties, fell in the attack on Quebec, 31st December 1775, aged 37 years."

A Note on Bibliography and Research

The documentary research on which this book is based was done in the Library of Congress, Washington, D.C., the library of the New-York Historical Society, the New York Public Library, and the Provincial Archives in the Musée Historique, Quebec. Materials consulted included a great many unpublished manuscripts, maps, sketches, periodicals and books, extending in date through the past two centuries.

Much of the written material, in both French and English, was colored or distorted by the passions of the time and by lapses of memory. This was the case with original documents such as letters and diaries, with recollections written long after the event, with official reports, and with articles and books based without discrimination upon them. From the writer's sifting, the following brief list of printed sources appears the most useful for readers who want to follow his path:

Alden, John Richard, *The American Revolution, 1775–1783.* New York, Harper & Brothers, 1954.

Bolton, Reginald P., *Washington Heights, Manhattan and Its Eventful Past.* New York, Dyckman Institute, 1924.

Bradley, Arthur G., *Lord Dorchester.* Toronto, Morang & Co., 1907.

Castonguay, Jacques, *The Unknown Fort.* Montréal, Les Éditions du Lévrier, 1965.

Cullum, G. W., "Biographical Sketch of Major-General Richard Montgomery of the Continental Army." (Pamphlet) 1876.

Dangerfield, George, *Chancellor Robert R. Livingston of New York, 1746–1813.* New York, Harcourt Brace & Company, 1960.

Faucher de Saint-Maurice, N. H. E., "Notes Pour Servir à l'Histoire du Général Richard Montgomery." (Pamphlet) Montréal, Eusèbe Senécal et fils, 1893.

Fitzpatrick, John C., ed., *The Writings of George Washington.* Washington, D.C., U.S. Government Printing Office, 1931–44.

Force, Peter, ed., *American Archives, Series 4.* Washington, D.C., 1837–46. (Printed under authorization of an act of Congress.)

Ford, Worthington C., *et al., Journals of the Continental Congress, 1774–1789.* Washington, D.C., U.S. Government Printing Office, 1904–37. Vols. 1775 & 1776.

French, Allen, *The First Year of the American Revolution.* Boston, Houghton Mifflin Company, 1934.

Hamilton, Edward P., *Lake Champlain and the Upper Hudson Valley.* Ticonderoga, N.Y., The Ticonderoga Association, 1959.

Hunt, Louise Livingston, "Biographical Notes Concerning General Richard Montgomery." Poughkeepsie, N.Y., *News* Printing House, 1876.

Institut Canadien de Québec, *Centenaire de l'assaut de Québec par les Américains, 31 décembre 1775.* Québec, A. Coté et cie., 1876. (Transcript of a commemorative meeting on the one-hundredth anniversary of the attack.)

Lossing, Benson J., *History of New York City.* New York, Perine Engraving and Publishing Co., 1884.

————— *The Life and Times of Philip Schuyler.* New York, Sheldon & Co., 1872–73.

Nettels, Curtis P., *George Washington and American Independence.* Boston, Little, Brown and Company, 1951.

Parkman, Francis, *Montcalm and Wolfe.* New York, Collier Books, 1962.

Roberts, Kenneth L., *March to Quebec.* New York, Doubleday, Doran and Company, 1938.

Stacey, C. P., *Quebec, 1759.* Toronto, The Macmillan Company of Canada, 1959.

Stokes, Isaac N. P., *Iconography of Manhattan Island, 1498–1909.* New York, R. H. Dodd, 1915–28.

Wood, William C. H., *The Father of British Canada.* Toronto, Glasgow, Brook & Co., 1916.

The author's research also included carefully retracing the steps taken by Richard Montgomery in 1775, from the site of

New York City in colonial times up the Hudson Valley, through the lake country to Fort Ticonderoga, Crown Point, St. John's Chambly, Montreal, and down the St. Lawrence River to the walls of Quebec. Though much is changed, an imaginative eye and a sense of history reveal a great many details as they must have appeared to Montgomery and his command when they passed through these places.

Index